HOME-MADE BABY TOYS

HOME-MADE BABY TOYS

SARA K. SWAN

DRAWINGS AND DESIGN BY
JAMES SWAN

PHOTOGRAPHS BY
BILL CAHILL

HOUGHTON MIFFLIN COMPANY BOSTON 1977

Copyright © 1977 by Sara Kidwell Swan
and James E. Swan

All rights reserved. No part of this work may be reproduced or transmitted in any form by any means, electronic or mechanical, including photocopying and recording, or by any information storage or retrieval system, without permission in writing from the publisher.

Library of Congress
Cataloging in Publication Data

Swan, Sara.
    Home-made baby toys.

    1. Toy making. I. Swan, Jim. II. Title
TT174.S9   745.59'2   76-48148
ISBN 0-395-25101-X

Printed in the United States of America
M 10 9 8 7 6 5 4 3 2 1

to my mother and father

CONTENTS

INTRODUCTION — 9

CHAPTER ONE — 17
THE EARLY WEEKS

CHAPTER TWO — 30
2 TO 3 MONTHS

CHAPTER THREE — 37
4 TO 7 MONTHS

CHAPTER FOUR — 51
8 TO 9 MONTHS

CHAPTER FIVE — 58
9 TO 12 MONTHS

CHAPTER SIX — 73
12 TO 18 MONTHS

CHAPTER SEVEN — 111
18 MONTHS TO TWO YEARS

TWO AND BEYOND — 126

INTRODUCTION

I am often bewildered by the things I see people buying in toy stores. Why, I ask myself, would someone buy a baby an expensive rattle when anyone could make ten rattles for the same price? Why spend five dollars for an imported carriage toy when you can make something more interesting out of a few beads and a length of sewing elastic?

It is not only the expense that concerns me. I am appalled at the quality of many toys for small children. Surely children's aesthetic judgment develops along with their cognitive abilities. Therefore, it seems important to give a child those toys which you as a parent find attractive and interesting and to avoid buying unaesthetic toys simply because they are inexpensive.

But when quality toys are too expensive, and the ones you can afford are poorly designed and not particularly appealing, you as new parents may find yourselves in something of a quandary. The only way out of this dilemma is to make the toys yourself. You will not only save money and give your child the kind of playthings that will encourage his mental and physical growth; you will also gain a good deal of personal satisfaction from participating creatively in your child's early development.

All the toys included here have been play-tested by my own child, Christopher, and most have been tested by other children as well. I have included approximate ages at which your child will probably enjoy each toy. This gives you an opportunity to prepare for future interests. But each child differs in both rate of development and play interests. Therefore, you should rely not on Gesell-type age norms, a toy manufacturer's notion of when your child should have what, or on what my child enjoyed at a particular age, but on your own observations of your own child. I found that setting aside specific periods during the day to sit down to observe Christopher as he played made designing his toys much easier.

When deciding what your child needs next, you should build on present skills and interests. A new toy should be familiar in some ways, but a little more challenging than the old one. Too much familiarity breeds boredom; too much challenge breeds frustration. A toy that is much too difficult only leads to feelings of inadequacy, especially if you try to force your child to play with it.

If you do make the mistake of giving him or her something too difficult, don't push it on the child or play with it yourself in hopes of providing inspiration. Just leave it on the shelf until the child becomes interested in it. When I first gave Christopher a home-made push toy, thinking it would substitute for chair-pushing, he ignored it at first, then became frightened as I exuberantly ran it around the floor. The more I tried to capture his interest, the more he avoided the contraption. Finally I gave up and left it in a corner, where he rediscovered it weeks later and pushed and pulled it around with enthusiasm.

I don't mean to suggest that you should never show your child how to use a new toy. On the contrary, I think it's a good idea to introduce it by showing in a simple, brief way how it works. There are also times when you may want to re-introduce an old toy by demonstrating a new way to use it.

If your child always uses nesting toys only for nesting, for example, you might sit down and build a tower with them. But you have to learn to withdraw quietly after you have shown a child once, and let the child take over in his or her own way. A child can only feel put down if you play "The Flight of the Bumblebee" on the xylophone when he or she can produce only a feeble "plonk."

MATERIALS

Most of the materials you will need are things people have around the house. It's a good idea to save anything that looks as though it could be used as a toy:
- Scraps of material as well as buttons, pieces of fringe, tassels, and other leftovers.
- Plastic things — containers, bottle caps, bottles, etc.
- Kitchen items such as jar lids, milk containers, and old cooking pots.
- Various pieces of hardware, like drawer pulls and hinges.
- Above all, cardboard — paper towel and toilet paper rolls, shirt cardboard, cartons,

boxes, and pieces of corrugated cardboard.

If you save things diligently, you will need to buy very little. Since many of the projects involve cardboard, however, you will definitely need:
- a mat knife
- a metal straight-edge (to guide the knife)
- a non-toxic glue (Elmer's Glue-All or Slomon's Sobo)
- 1" fabric tape (Mystik tape or Stix-On)
- clear Con-Tact paper (All cardboard things need to be covered, even when the directions don't say so specifically, to protect them from the inevitable chewing.)

The projects in this book are geared for the average parent; they involve no skills that the ordinary do-it-yourselfer doesn't possess. For this reason there is little carpentry required and no directions for making toy cars or trucks, riders, climbing equipment, pegboards, or anything else out of wood. Many of the toys made of cardboard can be made out of wood, however, if you have the requisite tools and skills.

SAFETY PRECAUTIONS

Since babies put everything in their mouths, you should never let them play with anything small enough to swallow. When the directions specify buttons, they should be at least 1½" in diameter. Any beads you use should be large wooden ones such as those made by Playskool, Holgate, or Milton Bradley for preschool children — at least 1" in diameter. Similarly, if you use spools, they should be the old wooden kind, so that a teething child cannot bite pieces out of them — they should be at least 1" in diameter and 1" high.

The mobiles for infants described in Chapter One are not for older babies. Be sure to move them well out of range or remove them altogether as soon as the baby starts reaching (about two months old).

When you use cord or elastic to suspend toys from the crib gym, use strong ¼" cord or ¼" sewing elastic, <u>not</u> elastic bands or thin elasticized cord.

Always be sure to check for sharp edges. Experiment with the toy yourself, feeling it all over, to be sure your baby cannot be cut or jabbed.

You should use non-toxic glue such as Elmer's Glue-All or Slomon's Sobo for gluing cardboard. For gluing lids on hard plastic containers you can use epoxy or acetone. Acetone, sold in plastics stores or hobby shops, forms a permanent chemical bond between two pieces of plastic that cannot come unglued. Epoxy is nearly as strong, but you need to be careful to wipe off any excess.

For painting wood, use <u>lead free</u> enamel. (If you paint pictures on cardboard, you can use water base paint since you will be covering it with clear Con-Tact paper.)

PHOTOGRAPH

Coat Hanger Mobile
God's Eyes Mobile
Bird Mobile
Crib Gym
Dowel Rattle

CHAPTER ONE

THE EARLY WEEKS

Even in their first month, babies require visual and aural, as well as tactual stimulation. Until only a few years ago it was generally assumed that infants responded to little more than their own insides and that their visual perception was limited to discriminating between light and darkness. However, in recent years researchers studying early infancy have considerably extended our knowledge of the perceptual and cognitive capabilities of infants.

On the day they are born normal babies will look all around, show a preference for the human face — particularly the eyes and forehead — and can even track a moving shape with their eyes for brief periods. According to Jerome Bruner, somewhat older infants can even distinguish half-tones of color and diagonals. Other researchers have found that they will look longer at a circular bull's-eye than at a striped square and show a preference for complex stimuli.

Most of the structures necessary for normal vision are present at birth, if undeveloped. The opportunity to look at interesting stimuli in the early weeks helps infants learn to use their vision system to focus on stimuli both near and far, resolve details in the stimuli, control the amount of light entering the eye, and efficiently follow movement.

Researchers have concentrated on visual perception because the organs for vision are more highly developed than those for the other senses, and visual capabilities develop faster than the other senses. However, babies also respond to sounds and rhythm, smell, and tactual and kinesthetic sensations from birth. One recent research project found that infants respond to the rhythm of their parents' voices; movie cameras recorded the infants' movements as the parents talked to them and showed the infants moving in tempo to their parents' speech.

Before babies begin handling objects, their world is essentially two-dimensional, and objects are probably perceived as globular masses, distinct from the background, but without differentiated qualities. As the weeks go by they learn from their various senses to construct a three-dimensional environment composed of objects outside themselves which they can manipulate and act upon.

Maturation by itself is not responsible for the development of infants' ability to perceive and respond to their environments. Infants who receive appropriate visual stimulation from the first weeks of life learn to reach for and grasp objects far earlier than those who spend their waking hours in a bland environment. True, infants seem to spend much of their time sleeping, but their waking periods are concentrated learning periods. When you consider the vast amount of learning that occurs between the day of birth and the third month, when a baby starts reaching for objects, you realize how important a stimulating environment is for your infant.

Mobiles made with coat hangers and bright household objects are easy to construct. Be sure to hang them in your baby's line of vision, however, not overhead until the tonic-neck-reflex disappears. (Newborn babies lie with their head to the side, facing one outstretched arm, while the other arm is curled up toward the shoulder. This tonic-neck-reflex disappears in a few weeks.) You should also try to hang the mobiles about eight inches from your baby's eyes, since for the first few weeks infants cannot focus well on objects more than eight inches away. If the objects on the mobile are lightweight — paper and cloth are good choices - they will move in slight breezes. (1)

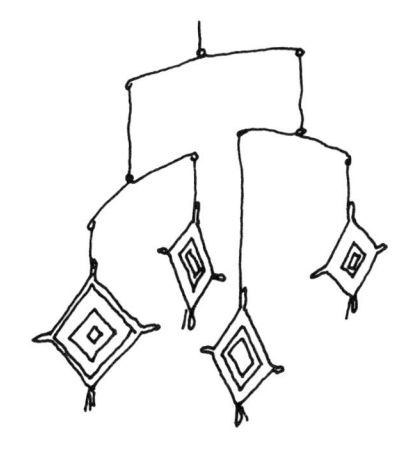

If you're more ambitious, you can make small "God's Eyes" using bright-colored yarn, small wooden sticks (such as those sold as hors d'oeuvres skewers, or the sticks from cotton swabs), and wire. (2)

You can use the leftover wire for another type of mobile. Bend it into a spiral and impale paper animals on it. The bird design in this chapter works well. (3)

Until babies begin to reach for objects, you can tape all kinds of things to the sides of their cribs. Use scraps of cloth in bold designs (such as stripes and polka dots), interesting magazine covers (particularly those showing a human face), a cardboard bull's-eye, bright-colored flags, a non-breakable mirror, or your own drawings.

Recent research with small babies suggests that they respond more to an intricate design in black and white than to a patch of undifferentiated color. Similarly, pastel colors will not interest a baby as much as strong contrasting colors. Objects that glitter or catch the light, a ball of aluminum foil hung from the crib bars, for instance, or metal objects like spoons, will also catch a small baby's attention.

As babies grow older, they will appreciate a hanging plant close by, a large clock (especially one with a second hand), or an aquarium next to the crib. Finally, don't forget other natural objects; spring flowers and fall leaves are as interesting as any man-made object.

It's not really necessary to buy any toys at this stage. If you have a music box or wind chimes, however, they provide pleasant aural stimulation for a restless baby. Alternatively, you can play records and (best of all) sing and talk to your baby.

After all, an infant's best source of stimulation is probably the parents, who provide ever-changing visual, tactual, and aural stimulation as they hold, feed, change, and talk to their baby. It is significant that the eight-inch focus range for an infant is about the distance from the nursing infant's eyes to the mother's face. The first thing infants recognize by sight is usually the mother (or the father, if he spends equal time holding the baby); after three or four weeks of studying their mothers' faces while they nurse, they smile in recognition. Shortly afterward, the parents' voices and the sight of familiar objects will also elicit infants' smiles.

A word of caution: don't over-stimulate your baby in your zeal to create an interesting environment. An over-stimulated child can become fretful and tired from too much excitement. One who is constantly barraged by a babble of voices and overwhelmed by too many mobiles and objects hanging around the crib will even learn to tune out stimulation rather than respond to it. The distinctiveness of the stimulation, rather than its quality, is what helps babies understand and relate to their environments.

Since babies become attached to familiar objects around their cribs, and can become worried when something new is substituted too quickly, it's a good idea to keep a familiar object in its place when adding a new one. You can phase out the old mobile or whatever once the baby becomes familiar with the new object. Sometimes removing a mobile for a while, then re-introducing it later in a new location can enhance its interest.

COAT HANGER MOBILE

<u>Materials</u>

    one wire coat hanger
    string
    paper, cardboard, cloth, etc.
    glue or cellophane tape

<u>Pinwheel (paper)</u>
1. Cut out square from colored paper.
2. Cut along dotted lines.
3. Connect four corners to center point with glue or small pieces of cellophane tape.
4. Attach string at center point with tape or by passing string through center hole and firmly knotting the end.

<u>Cardboard Sphere</u>
1. Cut two circles out of cardboard.
2. Cut along dotted lines.
3. Color sides differently or glue paper of different colors to circles.
4. Insert piece A into slot in piece B at right angles.
5. Tie string through hole.

Other Suggestions:

    animals made out of felt (appliqué decorations with glue)
    gathered pieces of cloth
    origami figures
    any light colorful material or object

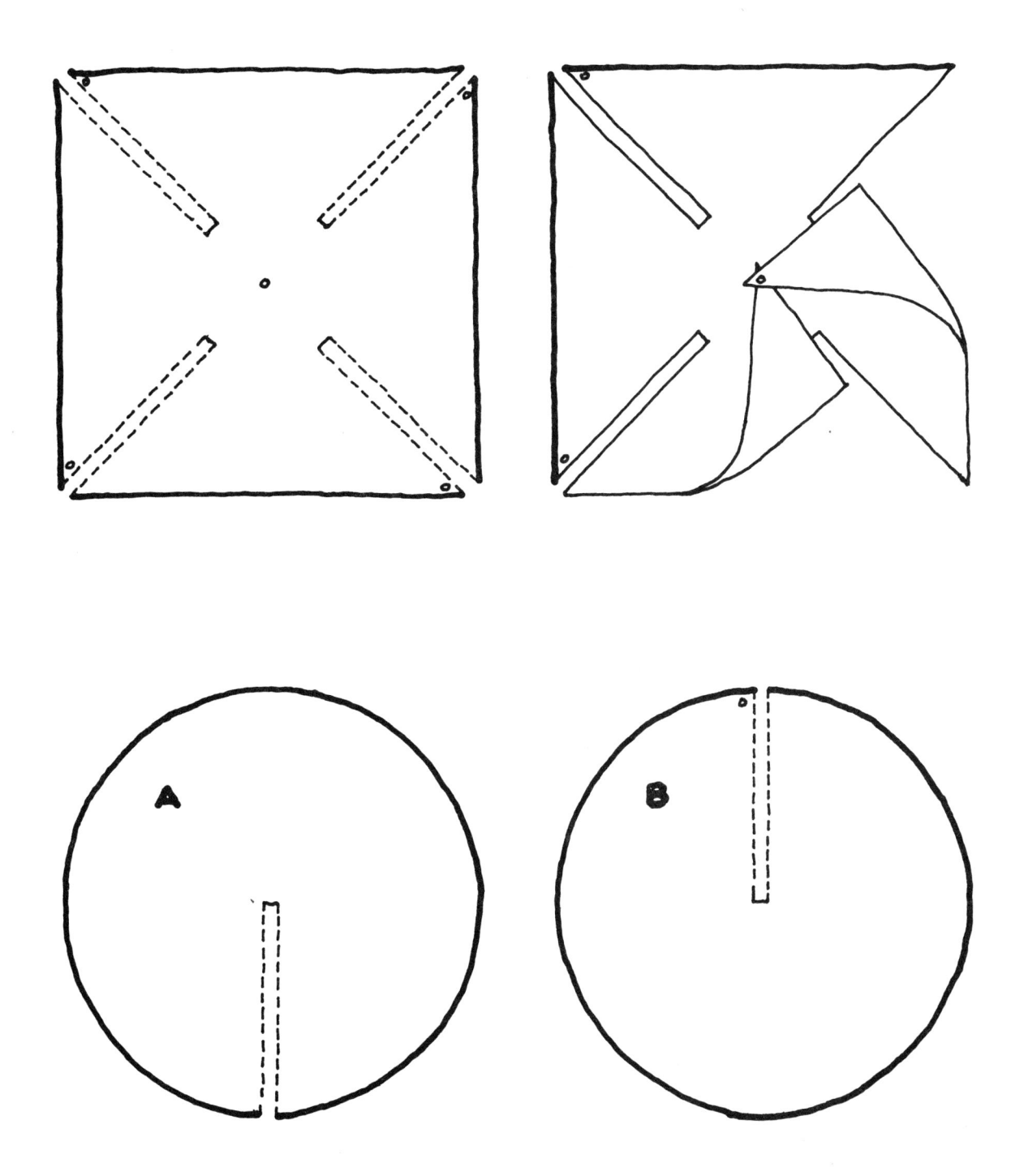

25

GOD'S EYES MOBILE

Materials

    colored yarn
    small wooden sticks (3" to 6" long)
    lengths of thin wire (stiff enough to carry the weight of the God's Eyes)

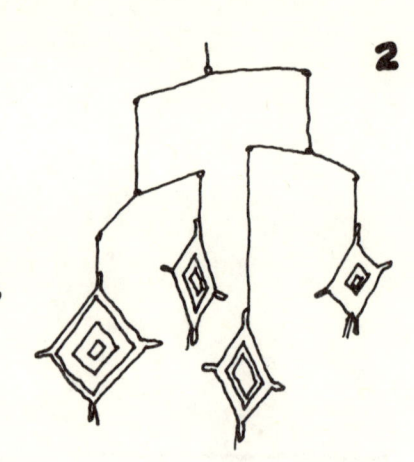

1. Tie each color yarn around crossing to secure sticks at right angles (A).
2. When using more than one color, start all colors at the center by tying them around the crossing. Lay the one(s) you aren't using along one stick and weave the color you wish to start with over it as you go around the square (B).
3. Weave in the direction shown (C), building up squares of color.
4. To change colors in the middle of the weaving, lay the first color along a stick and continue weaving with the second color, wrapping it around both the stick and the first color when you come around to it.
5. Tie off the last color on the stick opposite the one the extra colors lie along. Leave the yarn long enough to hang the God's Eye.
6. Trim the other colors to make tails (D).
7. When you have finished several God's Eyes (at least four) tie them to the ends of longer sticks or to lengths of wire and assemble.

27

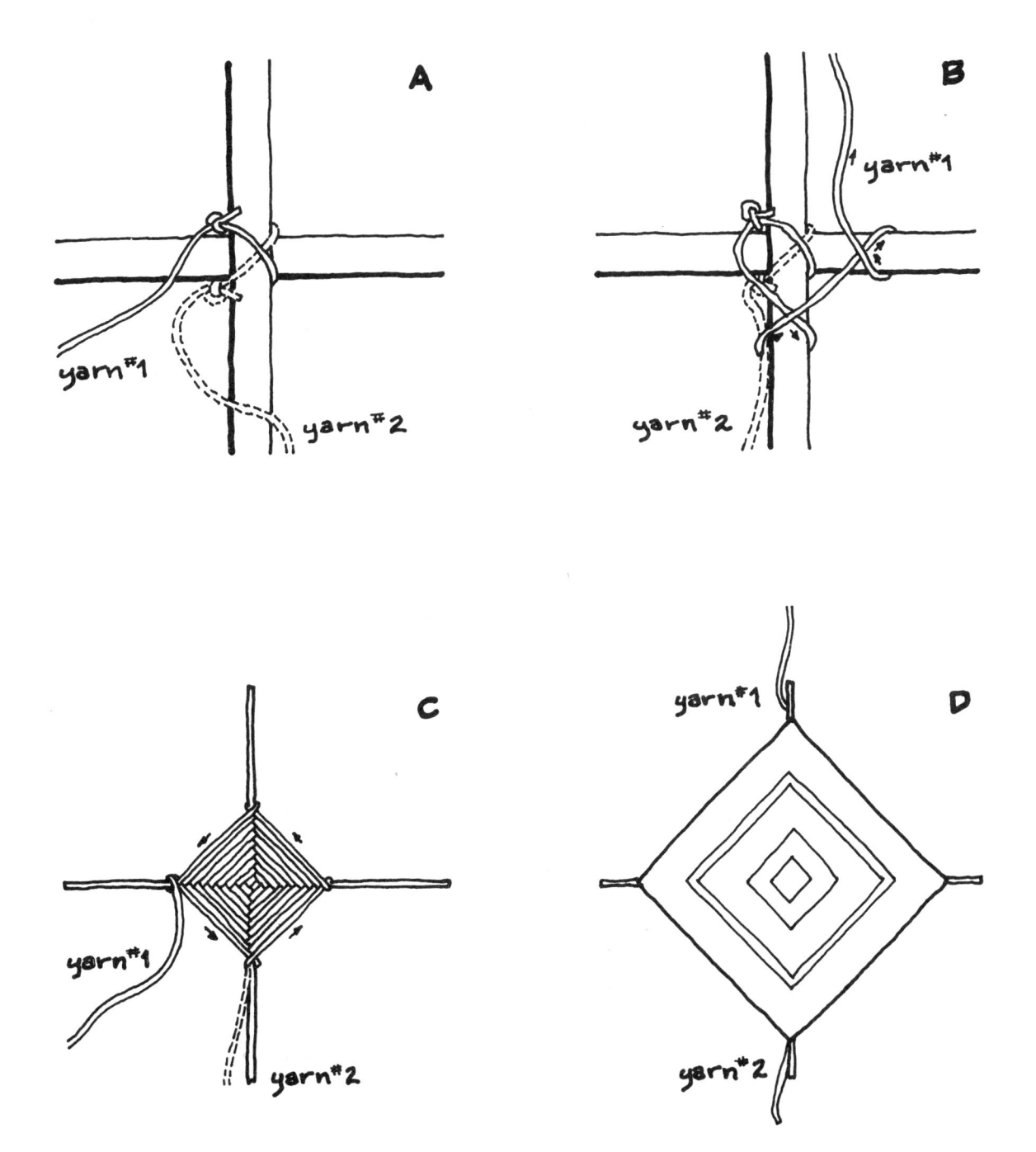

BIRD MOBILE

Materials

    lightweight paper (solid color or different color on each side)
    thin wire (should hold its shape when bent) 18" long
    glue for paper

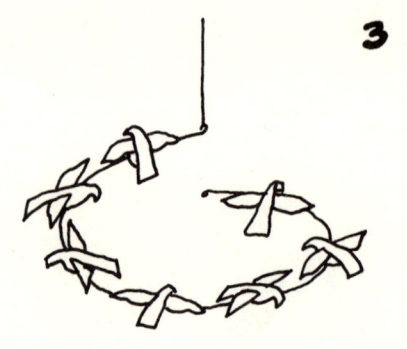

1. Cut six or seven birds out of the colored paper, using pattern to the right.
2. For each bird, put the left wing through the left slot and the right wing through the right slot.
3. Pull the wings all the way through.
4. Fold on fold line.
5. Glue the two sides of the head together.
6. Make dot or hole for the eye.
7. Gently bend wings between thumb and forefinger to make curve.
8. Work wire into a spiral with a loop on one end.
9. Impale each bird on wire through hole position shown.
10. Position birds along spiral and glue in place.
11. Hang wire from loop.

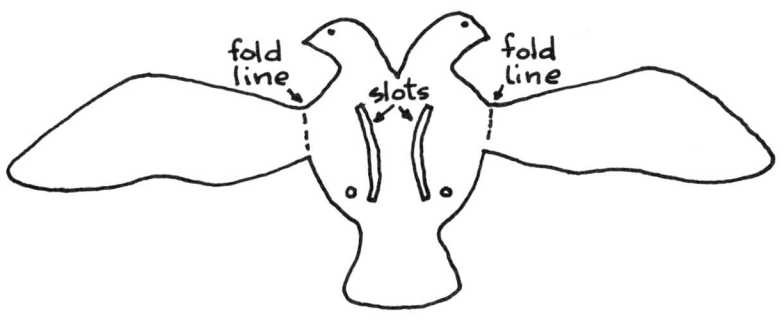

actual size pattern

CHAPTER TWO

2 TO 3 MONTHS

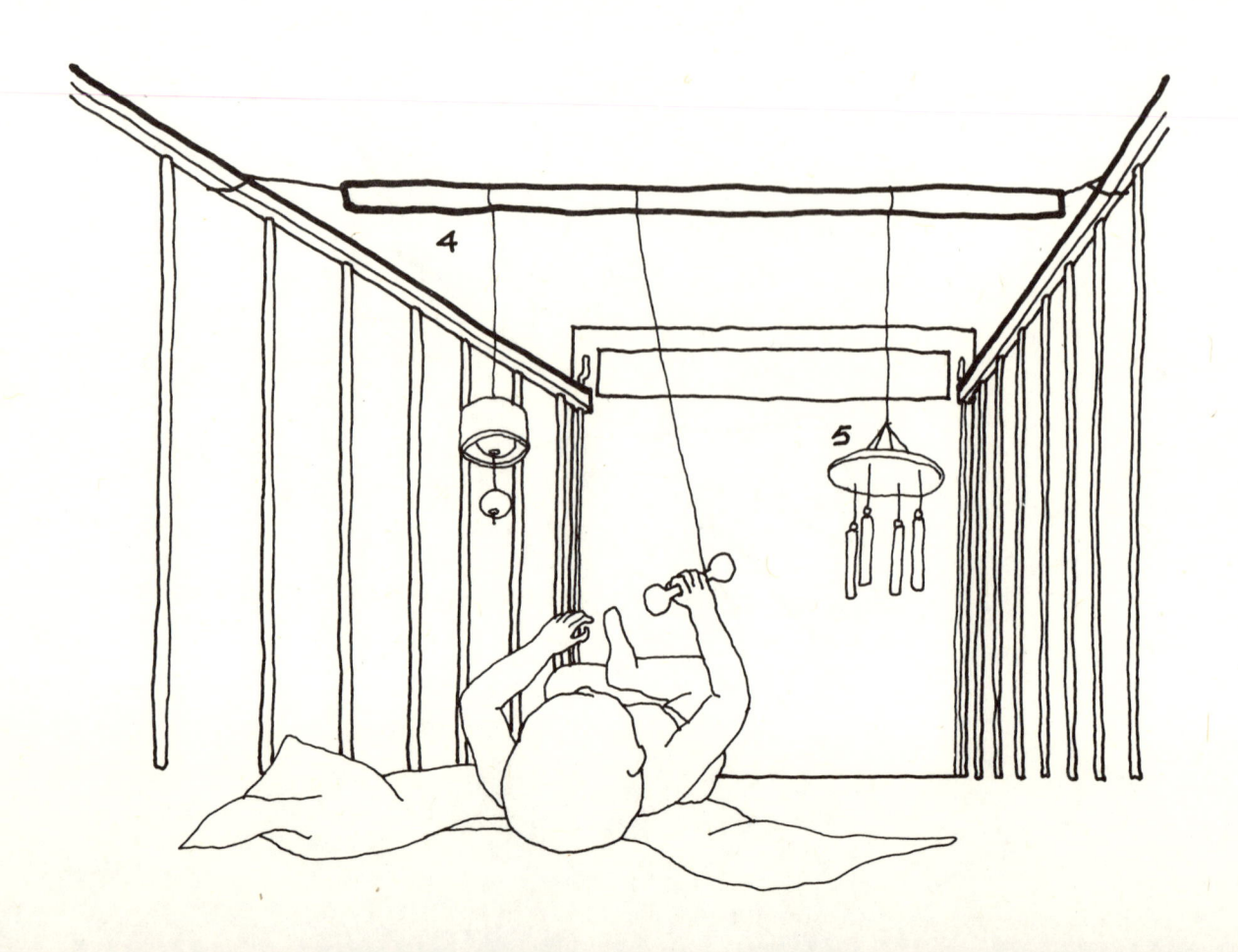

When babies begin to reach out for things, even though they can't grasp them yet, fragile mobiles must be moved out of range. Instead, you can hang objects on a strong cord stretched across the crib. It can be strengthened by passing it through a thin cardboard tube, if you have one. Or you may want to use a wooden dowel or a piece of broomstick with screw eyes in the ends. (4)

The advantage of the home-made crib gym over the store-bought variety is its adaptability. As your baby tires of objects, you can easily phase in new ones. In choosing objects for your crib gym try to provide a variety of experiences. Differences in color, texture, weight, hardness, and sound give babies an opportunity to discover more about their worlds and encourage them to use all senses. Here are a few suggestions:
- geometric shapes cut out of polyfoam and covered with different kinds of cloth
- cardboard shapes, flat or three-dimensional, covered with Con-Tact paper
- soft bath sponges tied in the middle
- felt animals
- circle bracelets (later the baby can grab onto them)

- <u>sturdy</u> bead necklaces made of 1" or larger beads
- knotted scarves
- cloth bows
- measuring spoons
- bells
- strings of large wooden beads
- a "dowel rattle" made of four dowels hung from a plastic container lid (5)
- safe pieces of hardware
- rattles, bought or home-made

When the baby learns to grasp objects, you can hang some of these on 1/4" sewing elastic so that he or she can pull them to the mouth and watch them jiggle when released. Bead people or animals strung on elasticized cord are especially interesting as a carriage toy.

When babies are gaining manual dexterity, rattles will encourage their endeavors. Since a "dumbbell" rattle is easiest to grasp and not expensive, it makes sense to buy one. Others you can make yourself.

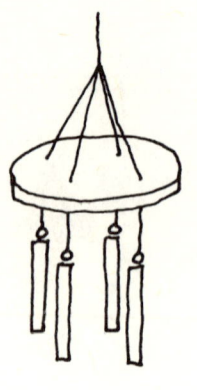

Fill plastic containers with dried peas, lentils, beads, bells, or whatever is handy, and glue the tops down very securely with epoxy or acetone. Wipe off the excess glue. Let dry overnight, then test to make sure you cannot pry the lids off. You can suspend these by passing yarn or cord through holes in the tops, or by making tiny macramé baskets of yarn. Remember to check the rattles often to make sure they are still glued tight.

The plastic bottle tops made for soda bottles can be tied together at the ring end and are fun to manipulate. You may also use tops from baby food jars. Punch holes in them and file down any rough edges (or pound around the holes with a hammer), then string them on a cord. Check to be sure you have eliminated all sharp edges.

You can make a bell-rattle using a plastic aerosol can cap and two large (1") beads. Pass a cord through a hole drilled in the cap and tie the beads on the end so that one acts as a clapper inside, while the other hangs below where the baby can tug and mouth it. Gourds, if you have some, also make good rattles.

Encourage your baby's interest in his or her feet, as well, by putting bright colored socks on them or bells sewn to circles of sewing elastic that fit around the feet. (Do not leave the baby alone with the bells on, in case they slip off.)

CRIB GYM

Materials
four feet of clothesline and a 1" diameter cardboard tube the width of the crib

<u>or</u>

broomstick (or thick dowel) about 3" shorter than the width of the crib, two screw eyes, and two short lengths of cord

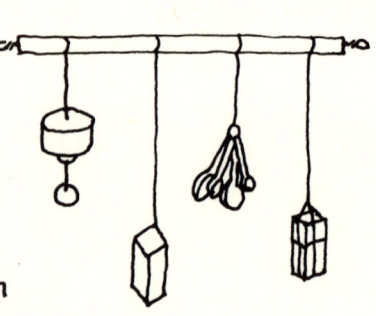

1. String the clothesline through the cardboard tube.
2. Tie it to each side of the crib.

<u>or</u>

1. Attach screw eyes to each end of broomstick.
2. Tie each end of broomstick, through screw eyes, to each side of the crib.

5

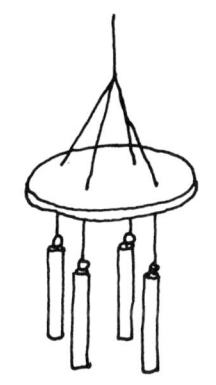

HANGING DOWEL RATTLE

Materials

- four 4" long enamel-painted dowels 3/8" in diameter
- four screw eyes
- plastic lid from coffee can or plastic container
- string

1. Screw one screw eye into the end of each dowel. Be sure they are screwed all the way in.
2. Firmly tie a piece of string to each screw eye.
3. Knot each string about 2" above the screw eye.
4. Make four holes in the lid, as shown.

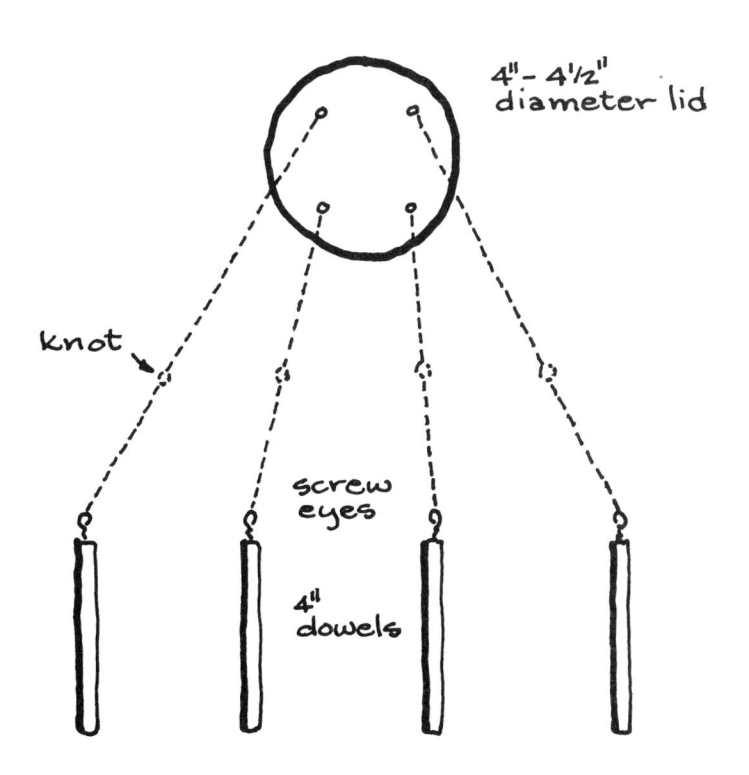

4" – 4½" diameter lid

knot

screw eyes

4" dowels

36

PHOTOGRAPH

Texture Pad
Texture Ball
Snake
Lizard

CHAPTER THREE

4 TO 7 MONTHS

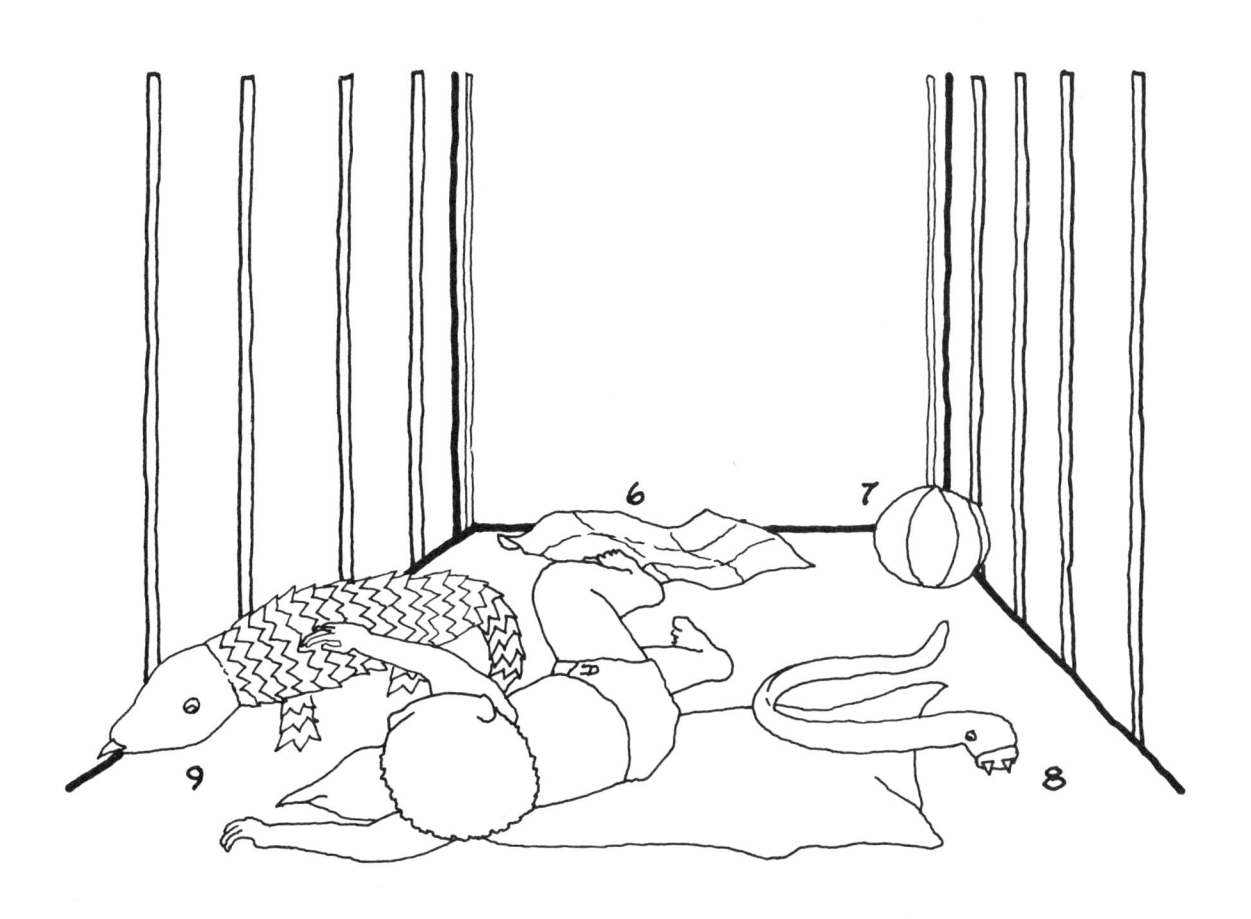

4 TO 5 MONTHS

As babies gradually learn to use their hands, they enjoy feeling and handling playthings. They crave a variety of tactual experiences.

Make a texture pad by sewing squares of interesting cloth on a diaper (6) or, if you're more ambitious, you can design a large pad to lie on covered with animals or people in different colors and textures. You might make it more three-dimensional by adding fluffy tails or floppy ears. You can also make a cloth texture ball stuffed with old stockings. (7)

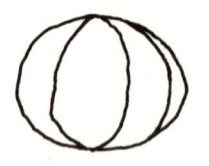

If you have leather scraps or pieces of vinyl, you can make simple animals. My child enjoyed chewing on a leather "spider." Other animals are easily fashioned out of children's socks, stuffed with cotton, stockings, or beans, and decorated appropriately with cloth, leather scraps, or yarn. Do not use buttons, since a child could easily swallow them. There are so many patterns available for making stuffed animals that I'm not including many here. When you've done a few using purchased patterns, you will probably find it easy to make up your own. If you do, it's a good idea to try out the pattern in muslin or another inexpensive fabric first. If you have scraps saved from other sewing projects, you can avoid buying material for stuffed toys. I had some cloth left over from hemming a pair of pants that made a great snake. I stuffed it with beans and sewed on some vinyl eyes and fangs. (8)

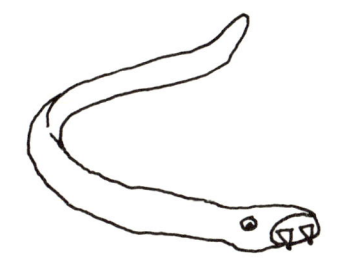

Scout around the house to see what else your baby would enjoy. Embroidered ribbon, sponges, an old hairpiece, pieces of fur, short knotted cord, samples of needlepoint, large wooden spools (by themselves or strung on cloth strips braided together), large plastic buttons (1 ½" diameter) strung on a cord, and small cardboard boxes are a few possibilities.

TEXTURE PAD

Materials

scraps of materials of different colors, textures, and patterns
a diaper

1. Cut out several squares of fabric, using pattern.
2. Hem each square.
3. Sew squares onto diaper about ½" apart.
4. Pin diaper to the crib sheet with diaper pins at each corner.

Or:

1. Sew each square to the next as when making a patchwork quilt.
2. Place face down on diaper and sew all around edge, leaving opening to turn.
3. Turn inside out and sew up opening.
4. Pin to crib sheet with diaper pins at each corner.

41

Pattern

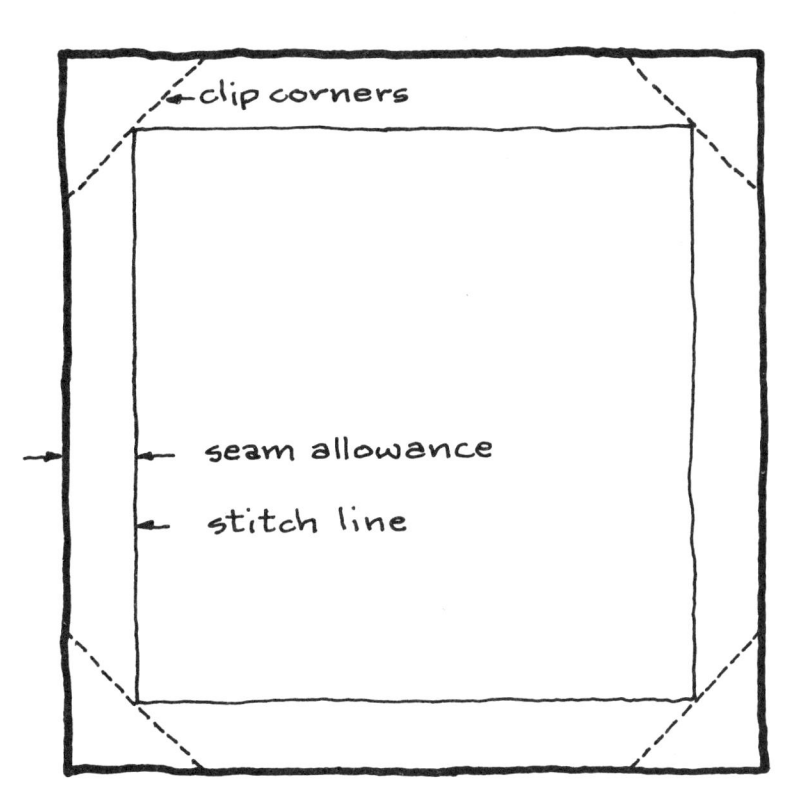

- clip corners
- seam allowance
- stitch line

Patchwork Pad
(suggested arrangement)

furry (fake fur)	slick (satin)	nappy (tweed)
directional (corduroy)	coarse (burlap)	soft (wool)
smooth (velvet)	metalic (lame)	tough (leather)

TEXTURE BALL

Materials

scraps of material – cloth, leather, etc. – with different colors, patterns stuffing material, such as old stockings or cotton.

1. Cut out of different fabrics six sections, using pattern A.
2. Sew sections together along seam lines, leaving opening for stuffing.
3. Turn inside out and stuff.
4. Sew up opening.

Makes a ball about 3½" in diameter.

To enlarge the pattern (diagram B):
1. Start with a perfect square drawn on tracing paper.
2. With a compass, draw arc AC using B as the radius point.
3. Draw diagonal of square BD to locate point E at the intersection of arc AC and diagonal BD.
4. Draw straight lines AE and EC.
5. Interpolate a curve from A to E between arc AE and the straight line AE, then from E to C between arc EC and the straight line EC. This is the curve needed for the pattern.
6. Add 3/8" seam allowance.
7. Fold square in half along fold line AC.
8. Cut out pattern along solid lines, cutting out both halves of pattern simultaneously.

Pattern A

seam allowance

stitch line

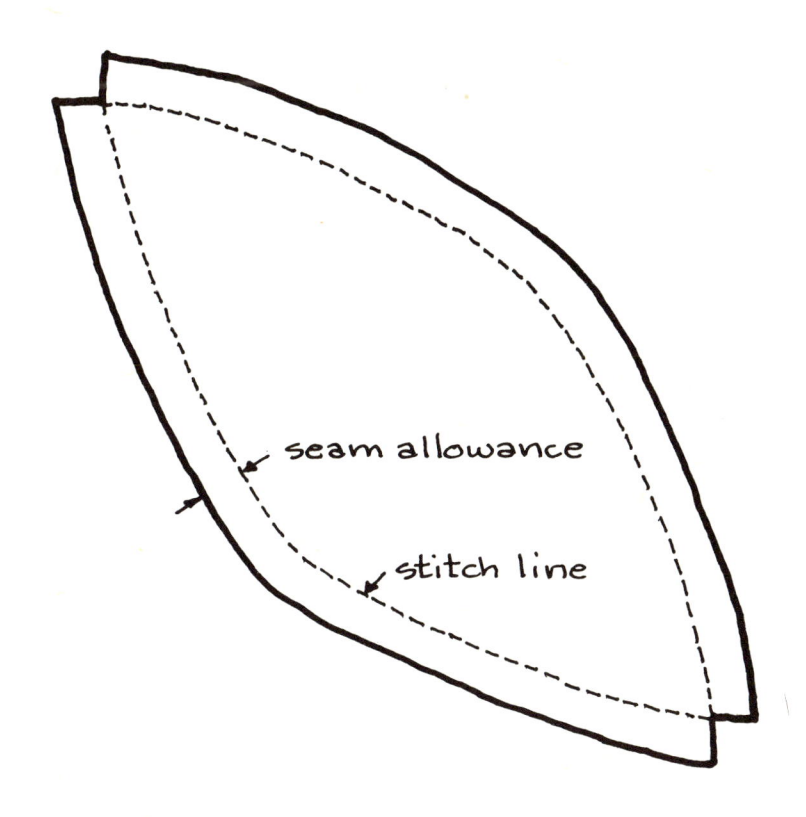

Diagram B

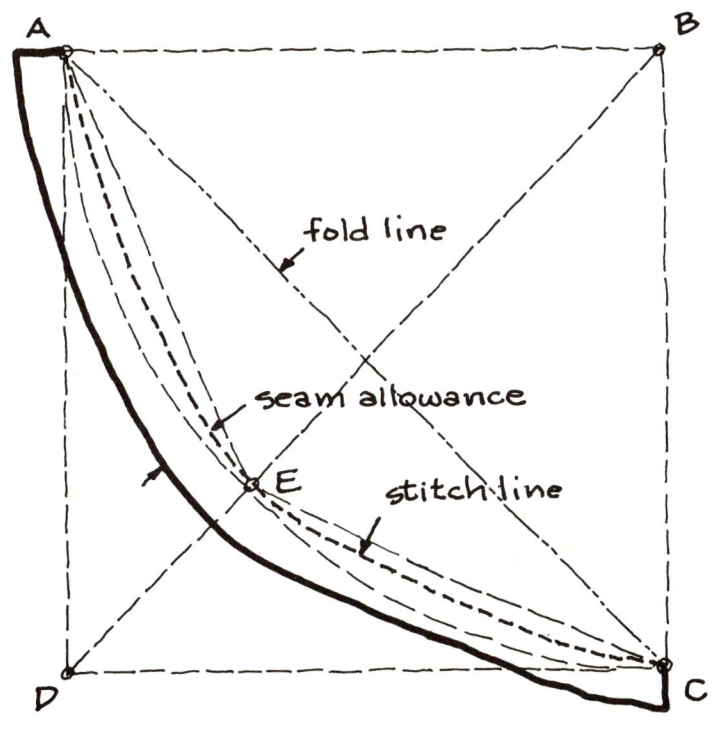

A — B

fold line

seam allowance

E

stitch line

D — C

SNAKE

Materials

fabric scrap 4" x 36"
vinyl or leather bits for mouth, eyes, and fangs
dried peas or lentils for stuffing

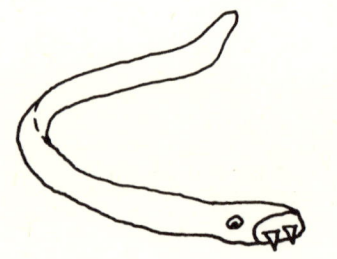

1. Enlarge pattern at right to desired size, using dotted squares as a guide.
2. Cut out pattern in chosen material.
3. Sew on stitch line with sewing machine set for small stitches (use strong thread), leaving mouth open to stuff.
4. Turn inside out
5. Stuff with dried peas or lentils. Stuffing should be loose enough to allow the snake to bend, but firm enough to prevent its being flaccid.
6. Sew vinyl oval for mouth to mouth opening.
7. Appliqué eyes and fangs.

Pattern for Top
(bottom identical)

mouth (red)

eyes (white, blue)

fangs (white)

seam allowance

stitch line

6 TO 7 MONTHS

By this time your baby may be ready for more complicated manipulative toys. Instead of providing single objects to grasp, try collections of objects in small containers. Collect different kinds of ribbon, jar tops, a set of sponge shapes, colored balls, some wooden shapes or beads or spools, corks of different sizes (unless the first teeth have appeared), a set of ring shapes (circle bracelets, napkin rings, large curtain rings, etc.), plastic cookie cutters, or whatever else you can think of. Put them in baskets, small cardboard boxes, or plastic containers and let the baby dump them out and handle them. In a very primitive way your baby is learning something about categorizing, while developing coordination. You can also categorize what you hang from the crib gym — hang a set of rings, or sound-makers, or shapes, isolating one characteristic at a time, so that the baby can compare differences in color, sound or shape.

Other small manipulative toys for this age are "books" made of cloth samples punched with a paper punch and tied with yarn, a Band-Aid box, cardboard boxes with flaps and holes cut in them, and a plastic bottle with ribbon and yarn that can be pulled out the top and out of holes cut in the sides (tape around the edges). You can also fill a clear plastic bottle with water, oil, and food color, and screw the top down firmly. Your baby will enjoy watching the bubbles as the bottle is turned around and upside down.

Babies also like handling large, lightweight objects that challenge them to coordinate the large muscles. You can provide a cardboard box, preferably with an interesting picture on it, a plastic jug with a large wooden bead inside or holes cut in it, or a large stuffed animal.

If you make a stuffed toy for this age, try to make it interesting rather than merely cuddly. I made Christopher a large lizard covered with shiny vinyl scales for him to ruffle up and peek under. (9) For eyes, use two circles of vinyl in contrasting colors, one large and one small. Sew the smaller one on top of the larger. Avoid using buttons, since they might come off.

Another good toy for developing dexterity with both hands is a "bendy" toy. Some toy stores sell rubber ones, but you can make your own by braiding cloth strips or yarn around bell wire (plastic-coated wire) and fashioning it into people or animals. Don't use any kind of rough rope, however, because it can cause a rash.

LIZARD

Materials

    1 yard solid color cloth
    ½ yard vinyl for scales
    vinyl scraps for eyes and tongue

1. Enlarge pattern at right to desired size, using dotted squares as a guide.
2. Pin pattern to folded material and cut along solid line.
3. Sew two sides together along back from nose to tail (use small stitches).
4. Cut out strips of vinyl scales and machine-stitch in parallel, overlapping strips to back and legs (if you are using a machine).
5. Cut out vinyl circles for eyes — one large white and one small dark for each eye.
6. Sew eyes to head.
7. With right sides together, sew bottom to sides along stitch line, leaving opening to turn.
8. Turn right side out and stuff with styrofoam pellets.
9. Sew up opening.
10. If sewing by hand, sew strips of scales to back and legs of lizard last.
11. Sew on vinyl tongue.

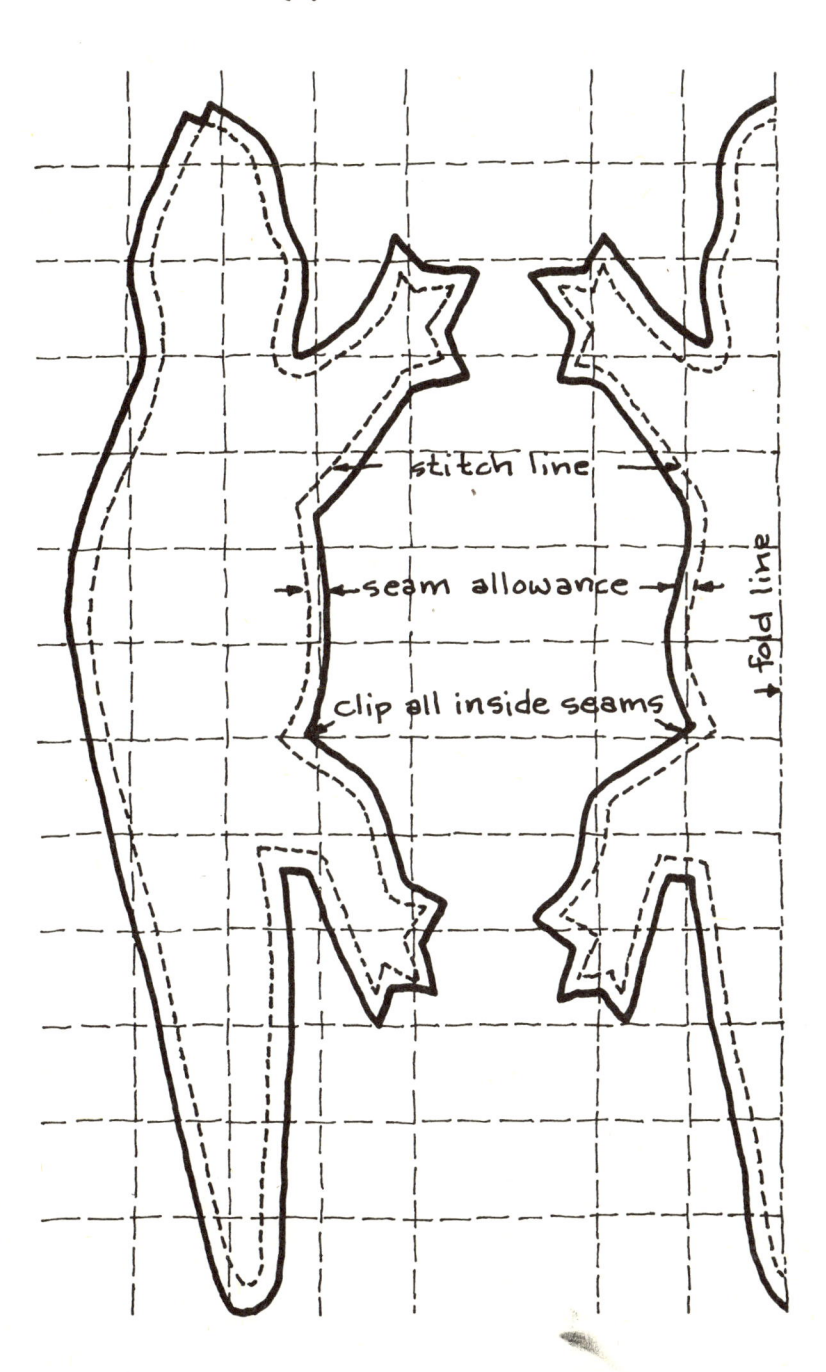

Pattern   Sides (2)   Bottom

- stitch line
- seam allowance
- clip all inside seams
- fold line

50

PHOTOGRAPH

Picture Board
Gear Board
Bottle Cap Holder
Cloth Books
Block Book

CHAPTER FOUR

8 TO 9 MONTHS

Sometime before nine months your baby may be learning to stand up. Mounting manipulative toys at chest height gives babies something to do while they are standing there trying to figure out how to get back down. One toy that worked well for us was a town scene painted on white matboard with doors and windows to open and close, clock hands and a windmill to turn, and a cart with wheels that went around. (10)

Another very successful toy of the same type is a hardware board, easily made by screwing whatever interesting pieces of hardware you have around to a piece of board mounted on the playpen or toy shelves. I used casters, a piece of shower curtain rod with shower curtain hooks, a hinge, a bureau drawer pull, a dead bolt, and the hasp from a padlock set. Be sure the pieces of hardware are safe, so that your child cannot be cut or pinched.

When your child begins to tire of the hardware board, you may want to make a board with interlocking gears mounted on it. You can cut a lot of them out of cardboard, using the pattern here, then laminate three or four of them together to make them thicker, and attach them with paper fasteners to a piece of sturdy cardboard (or use nuts and bolts to attach them to a board). (11)

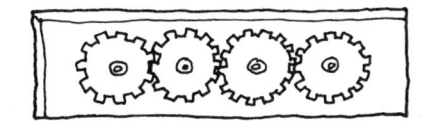

If this seems like a lot of effort, it's possible to buy a set of plastic gears, designed for four-to-ten-year-olds, which includes an eccentric wheel and a connecting rod as well as a number of gears. Mount a few of these for your baby now, and add more over time. Since this will last your child a few years, it is worth the investment.

As your baby learns to sit steadily in the bath tub, you will want to provide some bath toys. There is no need to buy special things. Plastic bottles and cups, funnels, pill bottles, sponges — anything that floats or holds water is fine.

PICTURE BOARD

Materials
- heavy cardboard (2½ sheets)
- fabric tape
- paper fasteners (long shanks)
- paints or collage material for pictures
- glue (Elmer's or Sobo)
- clear Con-Tact paper

1. Paint or make a collage of pictures on one sheet of cardboard. Include doors and windows, clock face, windmill, cart, or other vehicle.
2. Cut clock hands, wheels, sail for windmill, and any other movable parts, except doors and windows, out of extra ½ sheet of cardboard.
3. Cover with clear Con-Tact paper.
4. For windows and doors, cut through three sides of the opening. Score the back side of the hinge line without cutting all the way through. Reinforce with fabric tape on both sides of hinge and all around doors and windows.
5. To attach wheels, clock hands, windmill, sail, etc., make a round hole in the rotating piece large enough to allow it to rotate around paper fastener. Make another hole in the picture board. Insert paper fastener through both holes from the front. Splay the legs and tape them to the back of the picture board.
6. Glue or paint pictures on second

sheet of cardboard (backing) where doors and windows will open.
7. Glue picture board to backing, lining up doors and windows with the pictures on the backing.
8. Tape around outside edges of both boards to help hold them together.

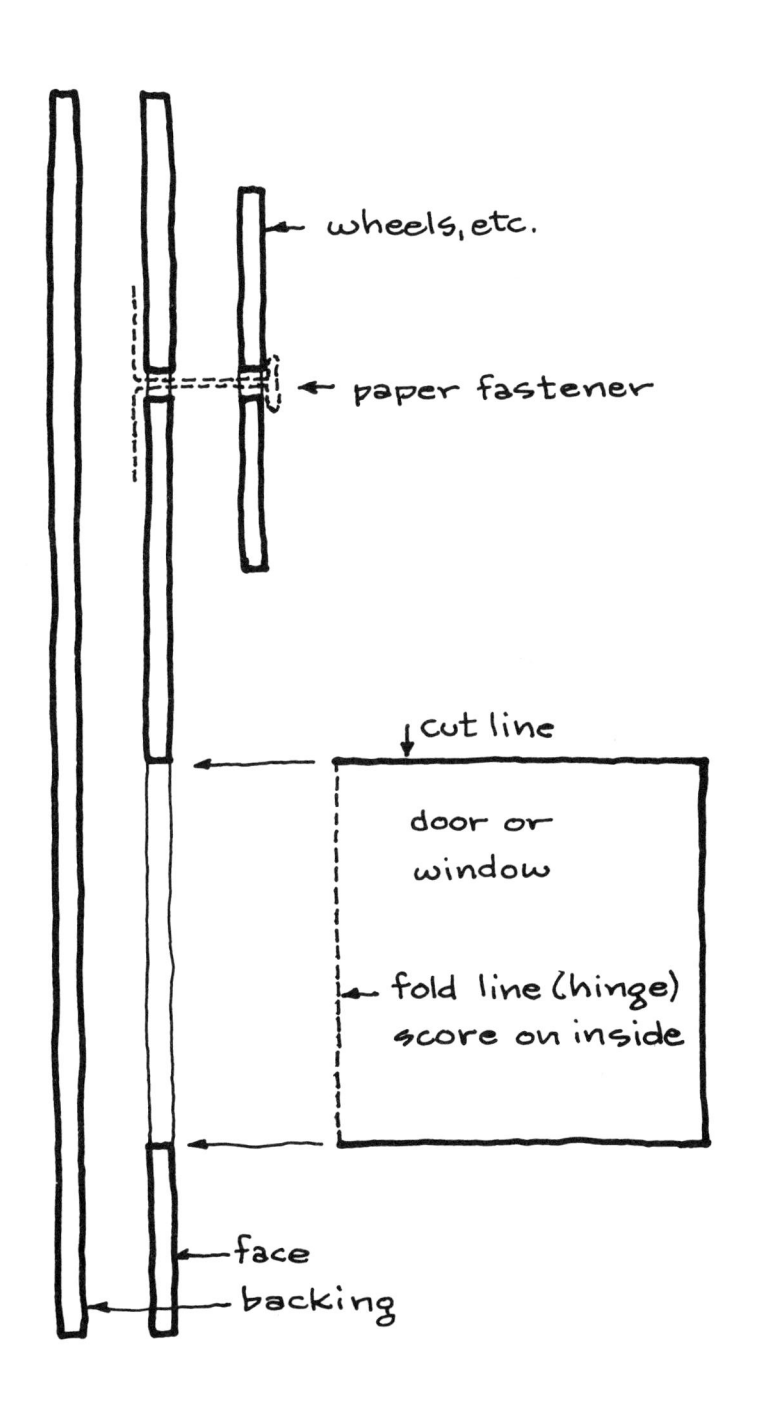

- wheels, etc.
- paper fastener
- cut line
- door or window
- fold line (hinge) score on inside
- face
- backing

GEAR BOARD

Materials

    heavy cardboard
    colored Con-Tact paper
    glue (Elmer's or Sobo)
    nuts, bolts, and washers
        or
    large paper fasteners

1. Out of heavy cardboard, cut the number of gears desired, using the pattern at right.
2. If cardboard is not heavy enough, laminate several gears together.
3. Cover gears with colored Con-Tact paper.
4. Cut out rectangle of heavy cardboard for backing and cover with Con-Tact paper.
5. Make holes in gears and backing and attach the gears to the backing with nuts, bolts, and washers as shown.
6. Tighten the two nuts against each other, leaving enough play for the gears to rotate.

Pattern

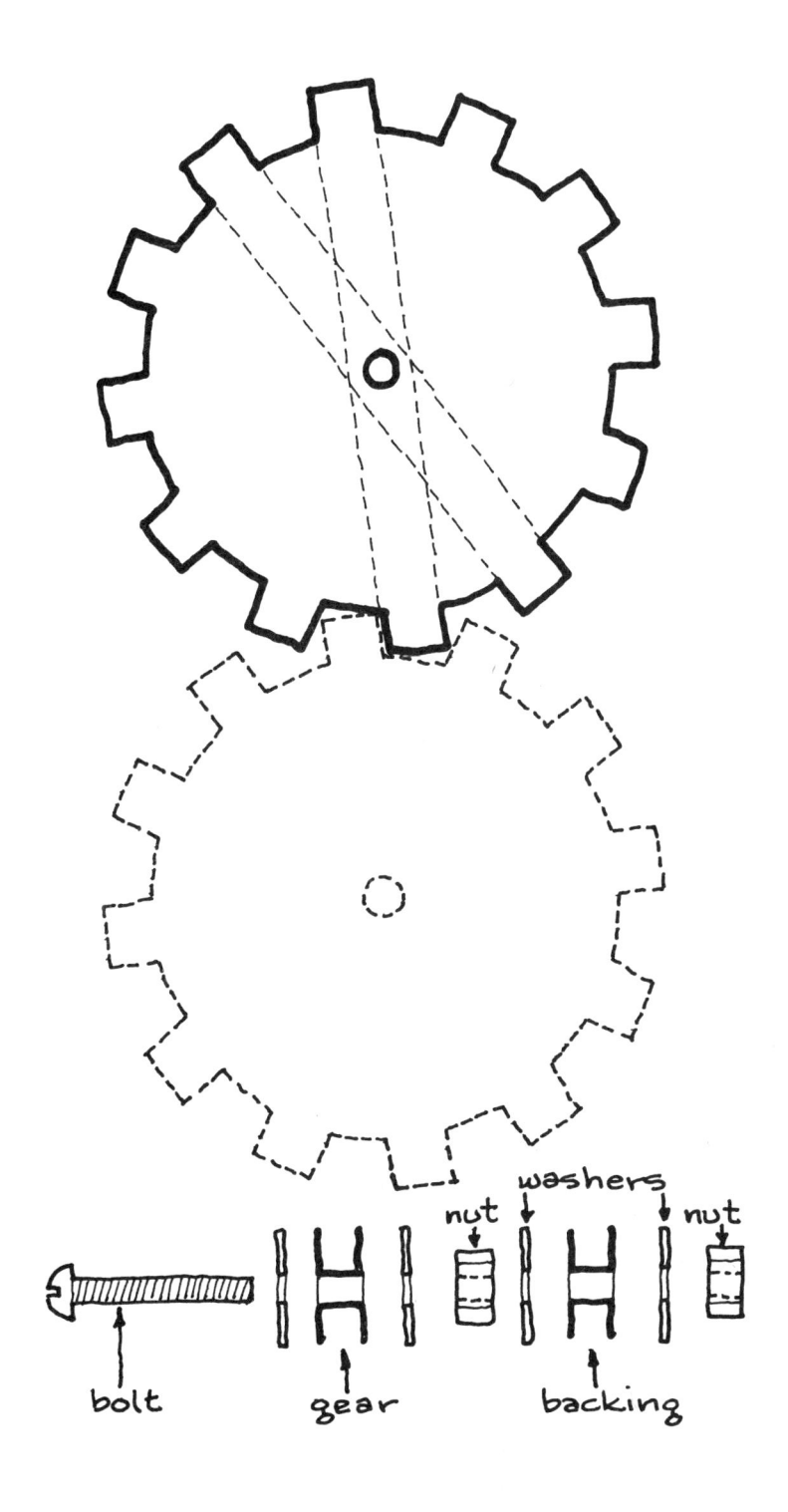

bolt · gear · nut · washers · backing · nut

CHAPTER FIVE

9 TO 12 MONTHS

Between nine and twelve months your child may be putting small objects <u>into</u> containers as well as dumping them out. In addition to the containers of beads, rings, and so forth you provided two or three months ago, you can add:
- a wastebasket of junk mail
- a cardboard box filled with smaller boxes (such as gelatin boxes, cereal boxes, cheese boxes), paper towel rolls, egg crates, and other containers you would otherwise discard. These are more interesting if you cut holes and flaps in them.
- clothespins in a wide-mouthed bottle

The kitchen may become an intriguing place at this age, especially if you put the safe things like pots and pans, wire whisks, wooden spoons, pastry blenders, plastic ice box dishes, loaf pans — you name it — on the lower shelves or in low drawers and let your baby investigate. Of course glassware, soap powders, and dangerous implements need to be moved out of reach and preferably out of sight. This may entail re-arranging the whole kitchen, but having a happy child in the kitchen when you're trying to get things done is worth it. If your child's interest begins to wane after a few weeks, you can set up an activity before you get involved in kitchen chores. For instance, set out a graded series of pots with lids and demonstrate how to take the lids off and put them back. Or hide a collection of small utensils in a set of pots and let the baby discover them.

As your child gradually becomes more adept, you need to provide putting-in-pulling-out games requiring more precision. A muffin tin is a good container for beads or plastic bottle caps. If there are just enough small objects to put one in each cup, the child is learning something (again, in a primitive way) about one-to-one correspondence, which is the basis of counting. You can use an egg crate or an extra ice cube tray instead of the muffin tin.

A toilet paper roll, or a towel roll cut down to size, makes a good holder for bottle caps or small balls if you cover it with Con-Tact paper and make a base out of wood or laminated cardboard to hold it upright. (12)

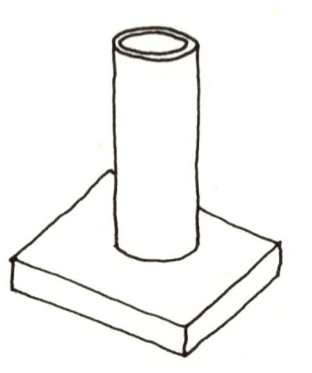

Christopher's collection of plastic bottle caps, incidentally, was one of his favorite possessions. He dumped them, put them in containers, teethed on them, rolled them, threw them, and fitted them together. Since they come in a variety of colors and shapes, they're also nice for a two- or three-year-old to sort and match, and for a four- or five-year-old to count and use in "attribute" guessing games involving size and color.

A few children enjoy a pounding bench at this age. Unless you're skilled at carpentry, this is hard to make yourself, but if you splurge a little and buy one, your child can put napkin rings over the pegs until he or she can use the hammer successfully. If the pegs are different colors, you can paint the rings to match so that your child can practice color matching at a later age. In the absence of napkin rings you can cut slices off a paper towel roll and paint them or cover them with colored fabric tape, or use the cardboard cores from the tape rolls.

Some children can also begin to make sense out of nesting toys at this age. Clear plastic pill bottles, if you have enough to make a series, are fine. Christopher used to love popping the tops off and fitting them back on, as well. Better still are the larger plastic salve jars with screw-on tops. Give your child the jars first, and add the tops at a later age. Jars that come in different sizes—some freeze-dried coffee jars, for instance—usually have graded lids that can be used for nesting. I wouldn't provide more than three cups in a nesting series at this stage. More than that becomes frustrating. If you have a large set of nesting objects, pick out the biggest, the smallest, and the one exactly in the middle to start with. Nesting toys should be perfectly graded, with equal increments between each one in the series, if your child is to see clearly the relationship of small, medium, and large.

A child this age often enjoys opening and closing boxes. A cigar box is perfect, especially if you put something inside. A set of pictures mounted on cardboard will fit easily into a cigar box, and they are useful for naming games. Or you can put the pictures in a recipe box or letter holder, although these are more difficult for a child to use.

If you find your child is interested in pictures, you can start making simple books. There are a variety of types you can try:
- "Junk mail" booklets. Punch holes with a paper punch and tie them together with yarn.
- Cloth books, if you like to sew. These are easier for a child to use if you stiffen the pages by sewing cardboard into them. (13)
- Pictures mounted on cardboard, bound with looseleaf rings or put into a small looseleaf notebook.
- Interesting photographs mounted on cardboard and protected by acetate report covers. Tape around the edges of the covers

to protect the photos from baby drool and the baby from the sharp corners, and bind them with loose-leaf rings.
- "Block" books of familiar objects. These are harder to make than the other types, but they're nice to hold and fun to stack if you make a few of them, and they are almost indestructible if you make them carefully. (14)

RAINY DAY PROJECTS

As your baby begins to sleep less during the daytime, being inside on a rainy day is harder to take. It helps to have special rainy day activities. We used to fill the baby bath with water and devoted half an hour to water play, using the bath toys and other objects I brought out just on rainy days. Putting old towels on the floor minimizes the danger of slipping.

Wet days are also a good time for short trips to special places. We had a toy center nearby with lots of space and large muscle apparatus where Christopher could play while I stole ideas for toys to make. A natural history museum or a large gymnasium are also fun to visit. Any large place where a child can move around fairly safely and explore new territory helps everyone forget the soggy weather. Occasionally, we invited another small child to play or went visiting. Later on, of course, when children begin walking around, rain no longer stops them from going outside and splashing in the puddles.

THE PLAY AREA

If your child is creeping and playing on the floor rather than in a playpen or crib, you need to set aside a space for the child's own play area. Use low shelves rather than a toy box for the toys so that your child can readily see what is there and can reach things easily. Since children need to understand and make sense out of their world, they enjoy an environment that stays neat and in order. Give some thought, then, to where things go on the shelves. Categorizing the toys according to a simple system will help your child choose what kind of toy he or she wants to play with. Our shelves were arranged so that the noisy, social toys were in a section at one end and the unstructured toys for observation and quiet play by oneself were at the other. Puzzles and other toys that required a certain amount of manual dexterity and concentration, and which could be used either alone or with a parent, were in the middle. When Christopher went to his shelves for a toy, he could make a choice, depending on his mood and what kind of activity he was interested in, simply by going to one section or another of his shelves. This let him make a choice physically, with his whole body, before he had a mental concept of making a choice.

In addition to the shelves, set aside another area in your child's play space for large motor toys like riders, trucks, and climbing equipment. A child between nine and twelve months usually likes a single step to climb on. I simply turned over a bookcase, and tucked a spread around it, to serve as both a step and a table. A rug on the floor will eliminate some of the inevitable bruises. A milk crate, if you can find one, can serve a variety of purposes — a table to work at standing up, a container for large objects, and a nest to climb into.

If you still have room in the play area, incorporate a soft area for resting and cuddling, using polyfoam pads, or a mattress, and some pillows.

BOTTLE CAP HOLDER

Materials

    cardboard tube (toilet paper roll or paper towel roll cut down to 5")
    heavy cardboard
    glue (Elmer's or Sobo)
    Con-Tact paper (clear or colored)
    fabric tape

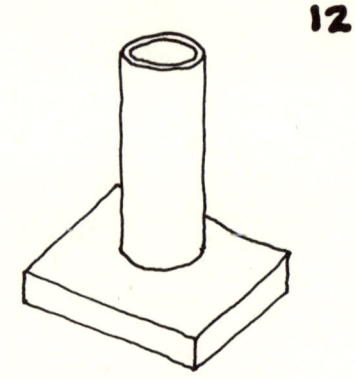

1. Cut four 4" squares of heavy cardboard.
2. Make a hole in the center of three of them slightly larger than the outside diameter of the cardboard tube.
3. Glue the four base pieces together.
4. Cover both the base and the tube with Con-Tact paper.
5. Glue the tube into the hole in the base.
6. Reinforce the top edge of the tube with extra Con-Tact paper or fabric tape.

67

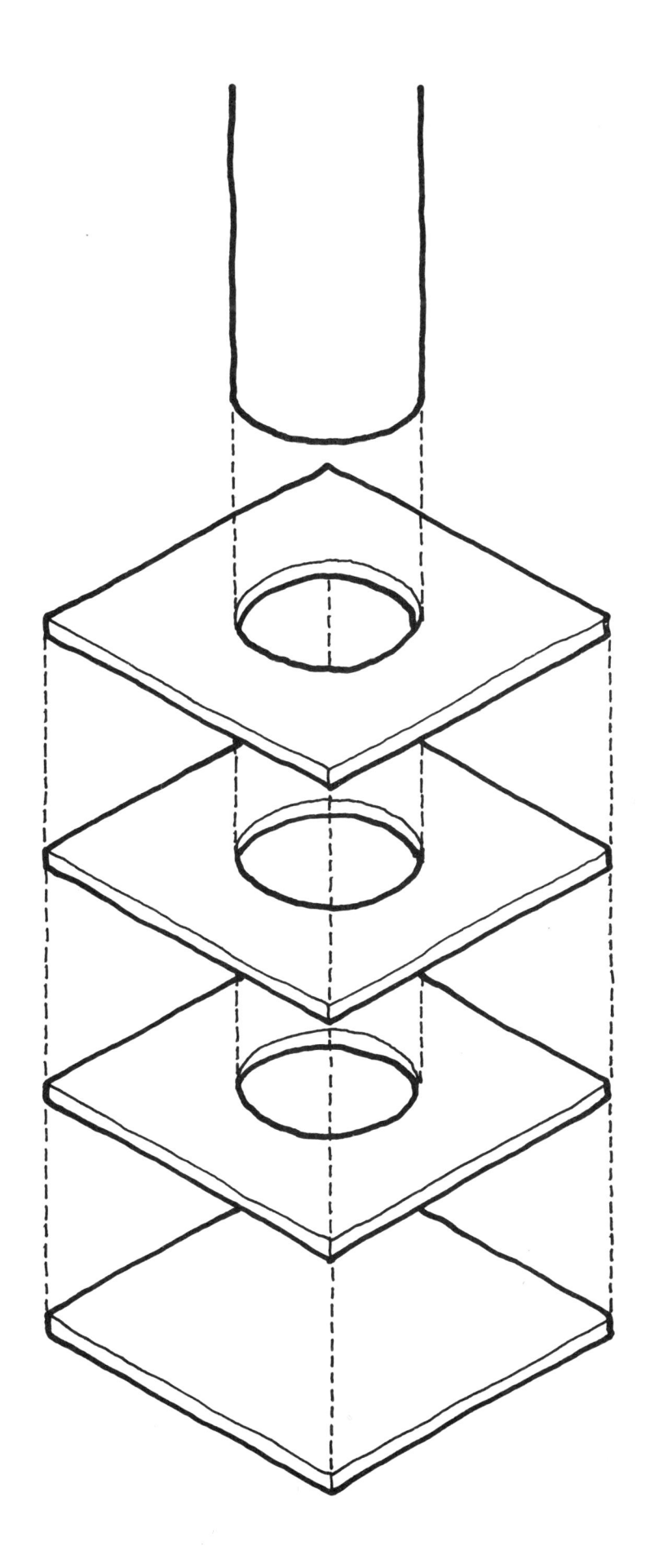

CLOTH BOOKS

Materials
- cloth for pages
- cardboard to stiffen pages
- optional: grommets and rings for binding, snaps, buttons, zippers, shoelaces, pictures, or any collage material

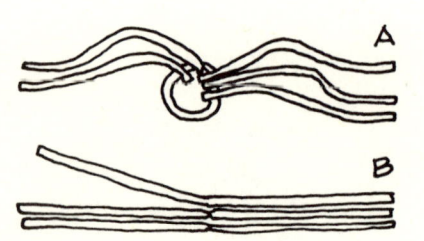

Simple Cloth Book (A)
1. Sew or paste pictures to pages, using stiff cloth.
2. Stitch around edges of pages to prevent raveling.
3. Make grommeted or stitched holes.
4. String pages together with yarn or rings.

Stiffened Cloth Book (B)
1. If pictures are to be sewn on, sew pictures to pages first.
2. Hem or bind edges of pages.
3. Cut out rectangles of cardboard somewhat smaller than pages, to allow for stitching.
4. Sandwich cardboard pieces between pages as shown, and stitch around outside.
5. Assemble pages on top of each other and stitch down the center line of all pages for binding hinge, as shown.
6. If pictures are to be glued on, glue them to pages of assembled book.

A stitch around edges — grommets or stitched holes

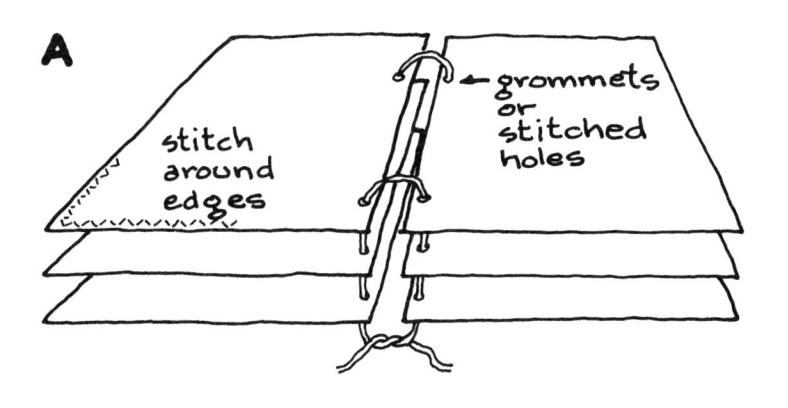

B stitch hinge through all pages

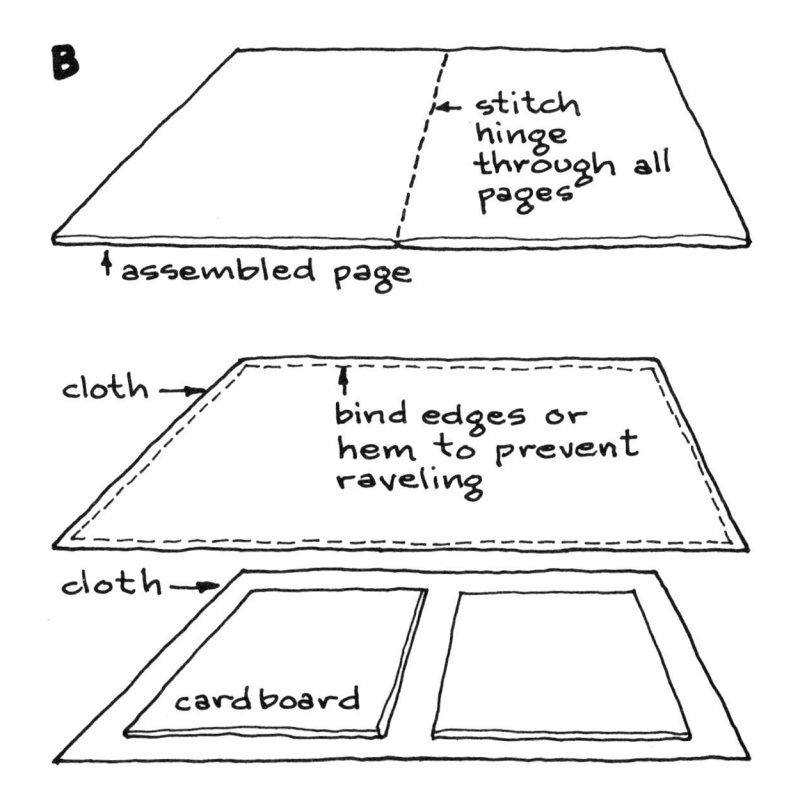

↑ assembled page

cloth → bind edges or hem to prevent raveling

cloth → cardboard

BLOCK BOOK

Materials

sixteen squares of cardboard (3" by 3" by 1/8")
fabric strip (jersey) (2½" by 22")
iron-on fabric (3" by 8")
fabric tape (3/4" wide)
clear Con-Tact paper

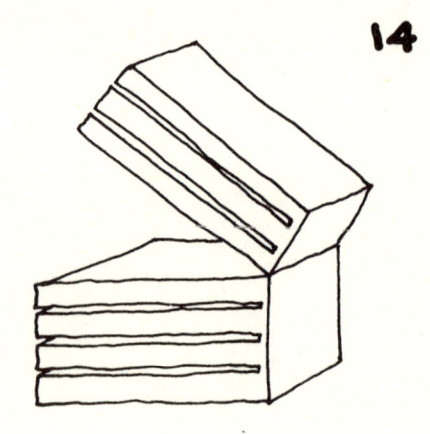

1. Draw or paint fourteen pictures, one per piece of cardboard, of your child's favorite objects, leaving two pieces for covers.
2. Cover each picture with Con-Tact paper.
3. Glue strip of jersey in and out of cardboard squares, as shown (A), to hold pages together. Jersey should be stretched somewhat taut as you go.
4. Glue (or iron) iron-on fabric around the outside of book, from one cover, around the binding, and over the other cover, as shown (B).
5. Decorate or title cover.
6. Cover with Con-Tact paper.
7. Tape all edges and the binding with fabric tape, as shown (C).

To make books of other sizes, use the following formulae:

jersey: number of pages (½" + page thickness) + 1"
iron-on: 2 (page width) + number of pages (page thickness)

note: "page" = single piece of cardboard

A
glue jersey
cover ↑

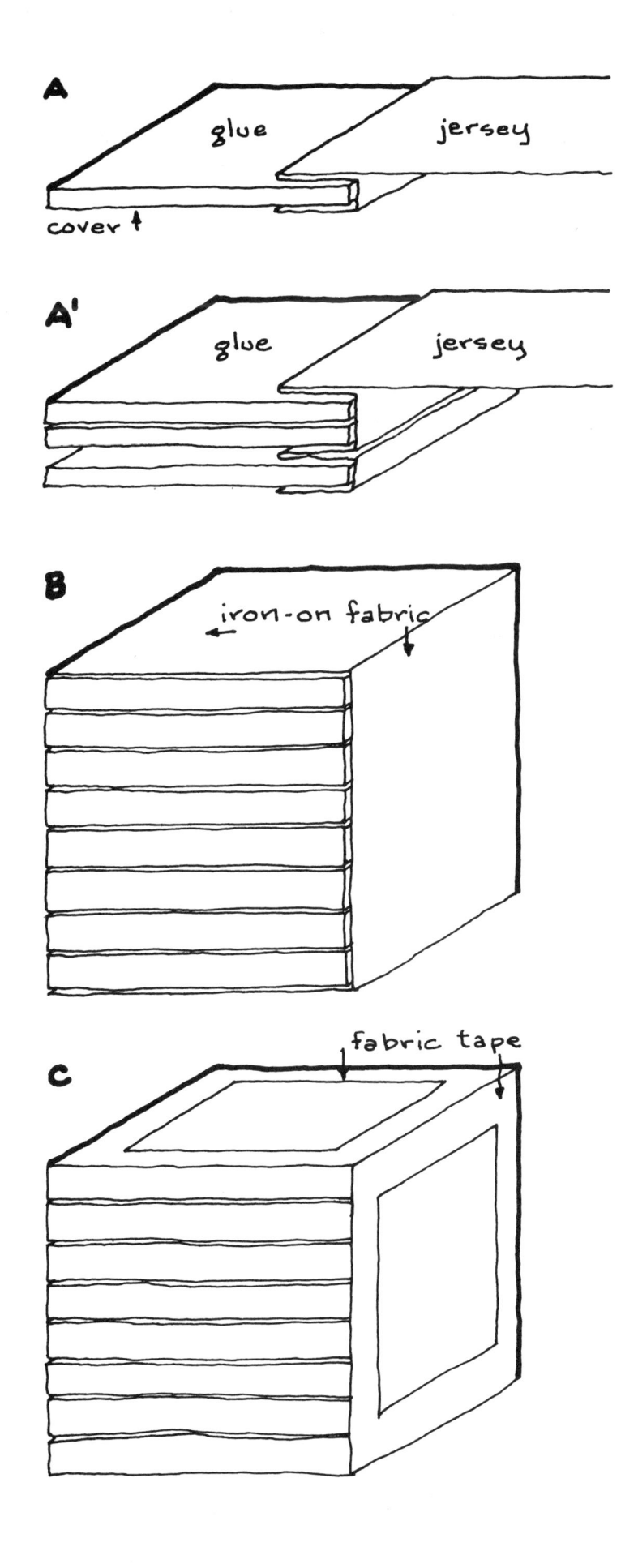

A'
glue jersey

B
iron-on fabric

C
fabric tape

72

PHOTOGRAPH

Shape Sorting Box
Sorting Board
Cylinder Inset
Push-Through
Cylinder Slide
Nesting Boxes
Soft Blocks

CHAPTER SIX

12 TO 18 MONTHS

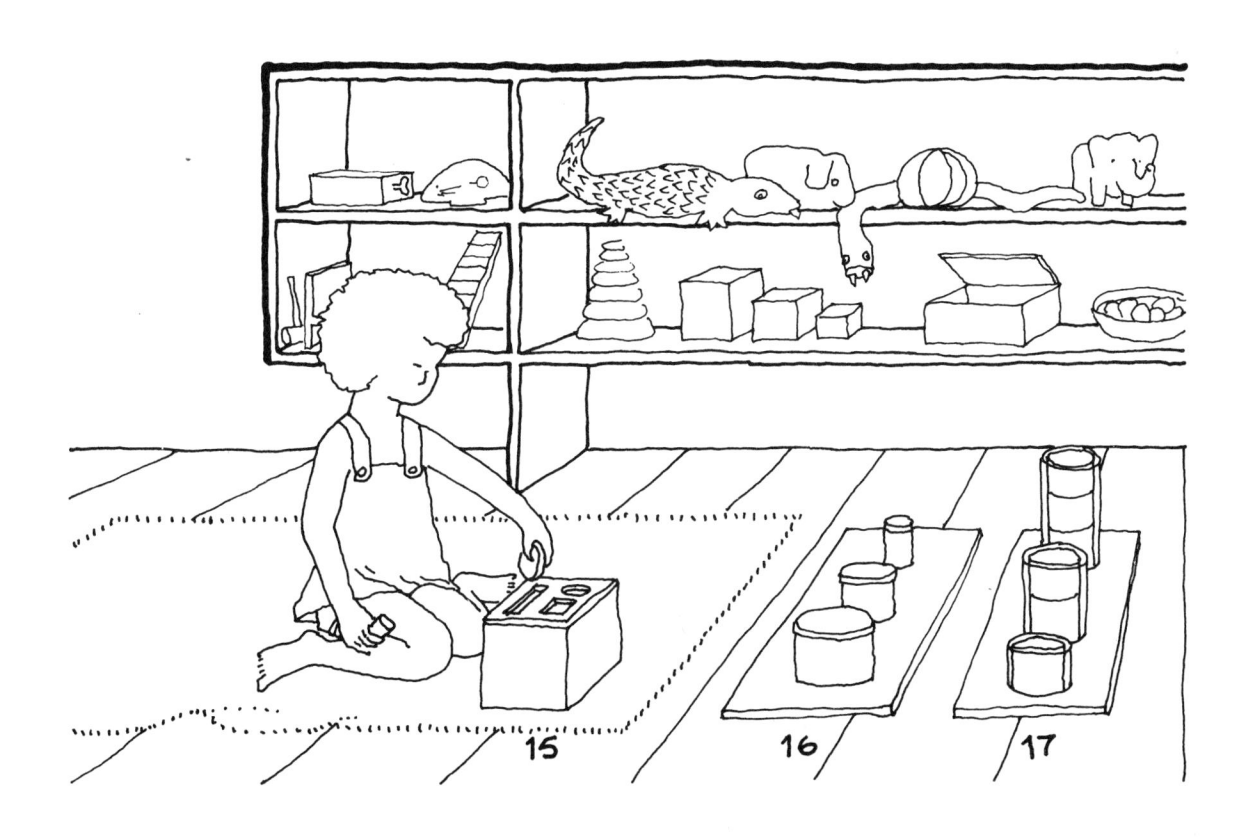

15   16   17

As children move into their second year, they need more complex manipulative toys, and more challenging large-muscle equipment.

EARLY PUZZLES

Most shape-sorting boxes available are too difficult for the one-year-old, but you can make one your child can manage, using no more than three shapes — square, circular, and oblong. In choosing objects to sort, make sure each fits into only the hole intended for it. I used blocks for the square hole, plastic bottle caps and spools for the circular hole, and film reels and jar lids for the oblong hole (really more of a slot). (15)

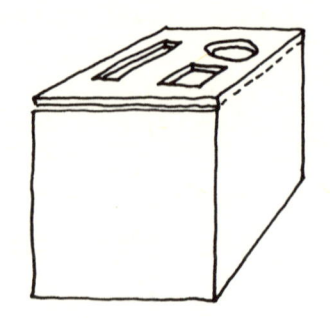

Another puzzle suitable for this age is a size-sorting board. You can use a set of nesting jars or cups for the puzzle pieces. If your child is ready, you could use four, rather than three, sizes. (16)

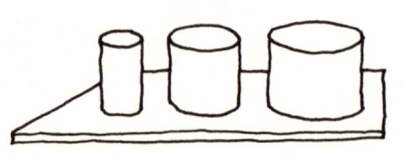

Finally, you can make a "cylinder inset." This is a toy that will grow with the child. For the small child it's simply a variation on putting-in-pulling-out toys. An older child will use it with more understanding of the concepts of size gradation it demonstrates. It will help the child conceptualize, in a concrete manner, the relationship between size and quantity. If the rings you used for putting over the pounding bench pegs are all the same size, you can use those in the cylinder inset, or you can cut more from paper towel rolls, or use the cores from empty tape rolls. These go into clear plastic cylinders graded in height so that the first holds one ring, the second holds two, and the third holds three. With luck you may be able to find clear plastic bottles in the right size. Otherwise, you can get a plastic cylinder of the right diameter and have it cut into the lengths you need. These will fit into holes in the base, which you construct out of cardboard. You may wish to make tops for the cylinders out of extra cardboard. (17)

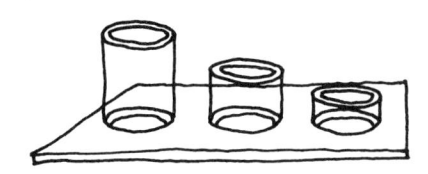

SHAPE SORTING BOX

<u>Materials</u>
    1/8" thick cardboard
    glue
    scrap of jersey
    1" wide fabric tape
    colored paper and clear Con-Tact
    <u>or</u> colored Con-Tact paper

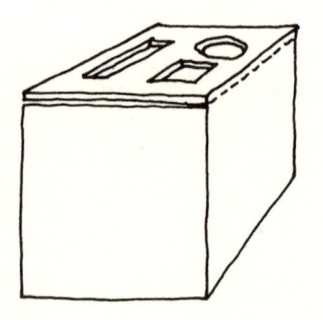

1. Cut out cardboard for inner box:
   four sides — 5 5/8" by 5 1/2"
   top and bottom — 5 3/4" by 5 3/4"
2. Glue four sides and bottom of the inner box together as shown (A).
3. Reinforce along all edges with tape, and let glue dry.
4. Cut out cardboard for outer box:
   four sides — 5 7/8" by 5 3/4"
   top and bottom — 6" by 6"
5. Glue the four sides and bottom of the outer box onto the inner box, gluing strip of jersey inside inner and outer box on one upper edge, as shown (B).
6. Laminate the two top pieces together, gluing the strip of jersey in between one edge to act as a hinge (C).
7. Cut holes in the lid to accommodate objects to be sorted.
8. Cover outside with colored paper and clear Con-Tact paper, or with colored Con-Tact paper.
9. Tape all joints and corners, including hinge edge and object holes (D).

77

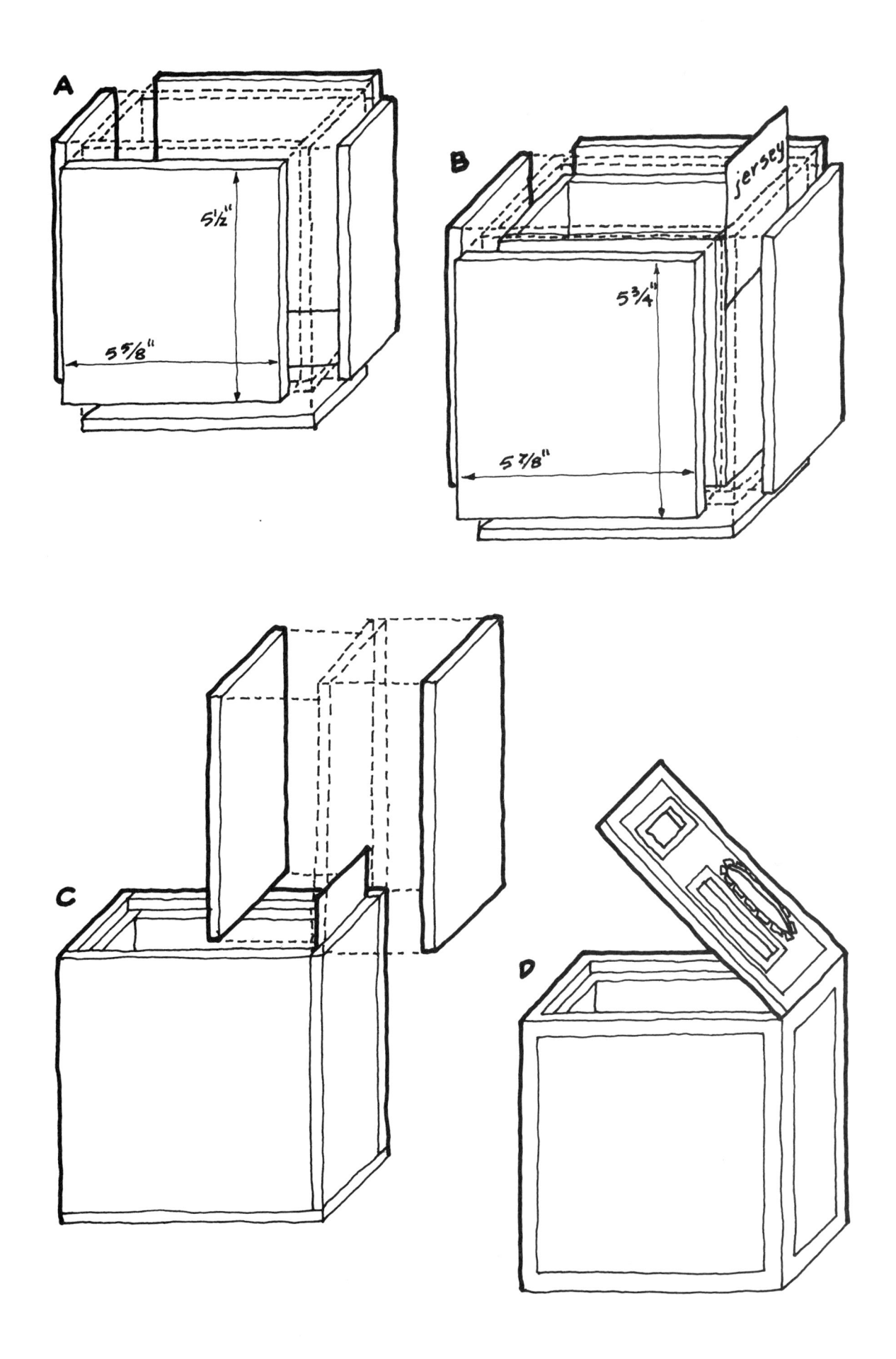

SORTING BOARD

Materials
- ⅛" cardboard
- set of three nesting jars or cups
- glue
- Con-Tact paper
- fabric tape

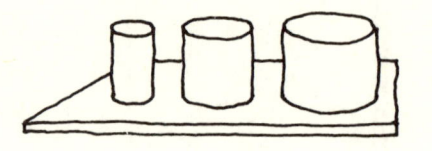

1. Cut out four rectangles of cardboard large enough to accommodate the three cups plus 1" between them and 1" on each end.
2. Cut out holes in three of the pieces of cardboard slightly larger than each of the three cups.
3. Laminate the three pieces together.
4. Tape around holes.
5. Glue the three top pieces to the fourth (base) piece.
6. Cover with Con-Tact paper.
7. Tape around the four edges.

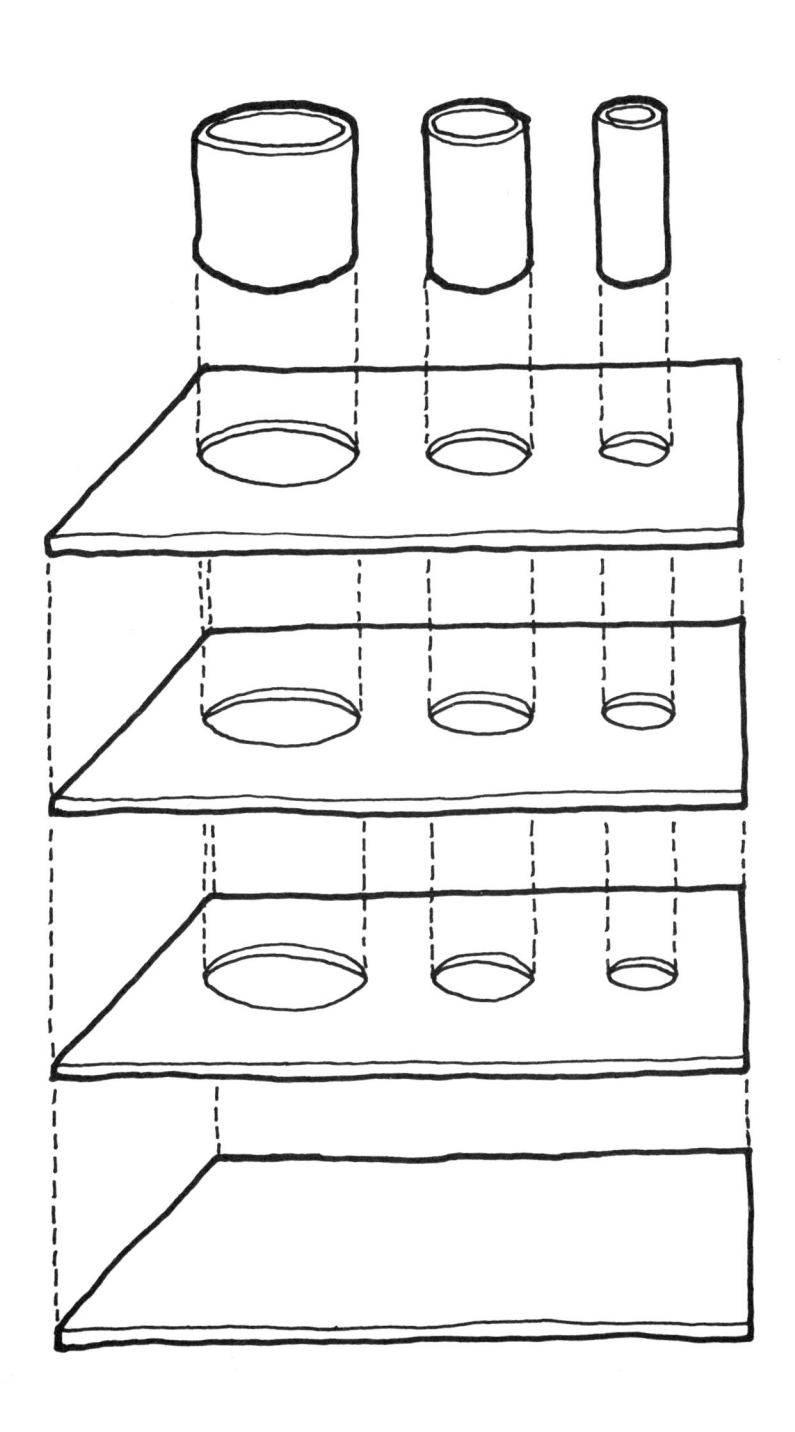

CYLINDER INSET

Materials

    1/8" cardboard
    plastic cylinder (diameter somewhat larger than diameter of rings)
    six rings (cores of 1" tape rolls, napkin rings, sections from paper towel rolls)
    glue
    Con-Tact paper
    fabric tape

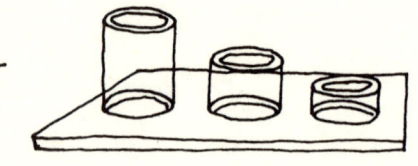

1. Have plastic cylinder cut to size so that three rings will fit in the first, two will fit in the second, one will fit in the third. (Or use clear plastic containers.)
2. Cut four rectangles of cardboard to accommodate three cylinders, plus 1" in between each and 1" on each end.
3. Cut three holes in three of the rectangles, slightly larger than the diameter of the cylinder.
4. Laminate the three pieces of cardboard together.
5. Tape around holes.
6. Glue the top three pieces to the fourth (base) piece.
7. Cover with Con-Tact paper.
8. Tape around all edges.
9. Cover rings with colored Con-Tact paper or colored tape: three of color #1, two of color #2, one of color #3.

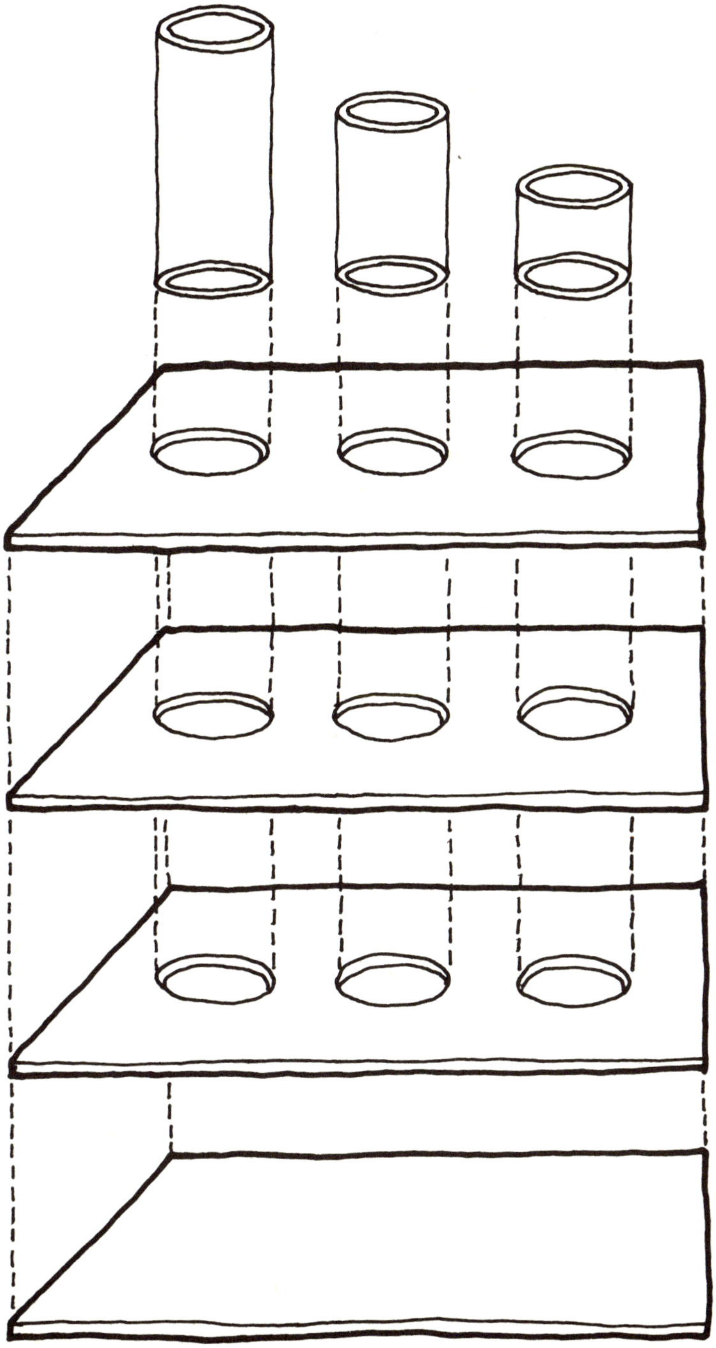

The next two toys don't seem to fit into any category, except that both give the child a chance to practice a bit of "magic" while discovering something about basic laws of physics.

PUSH-THROUGH

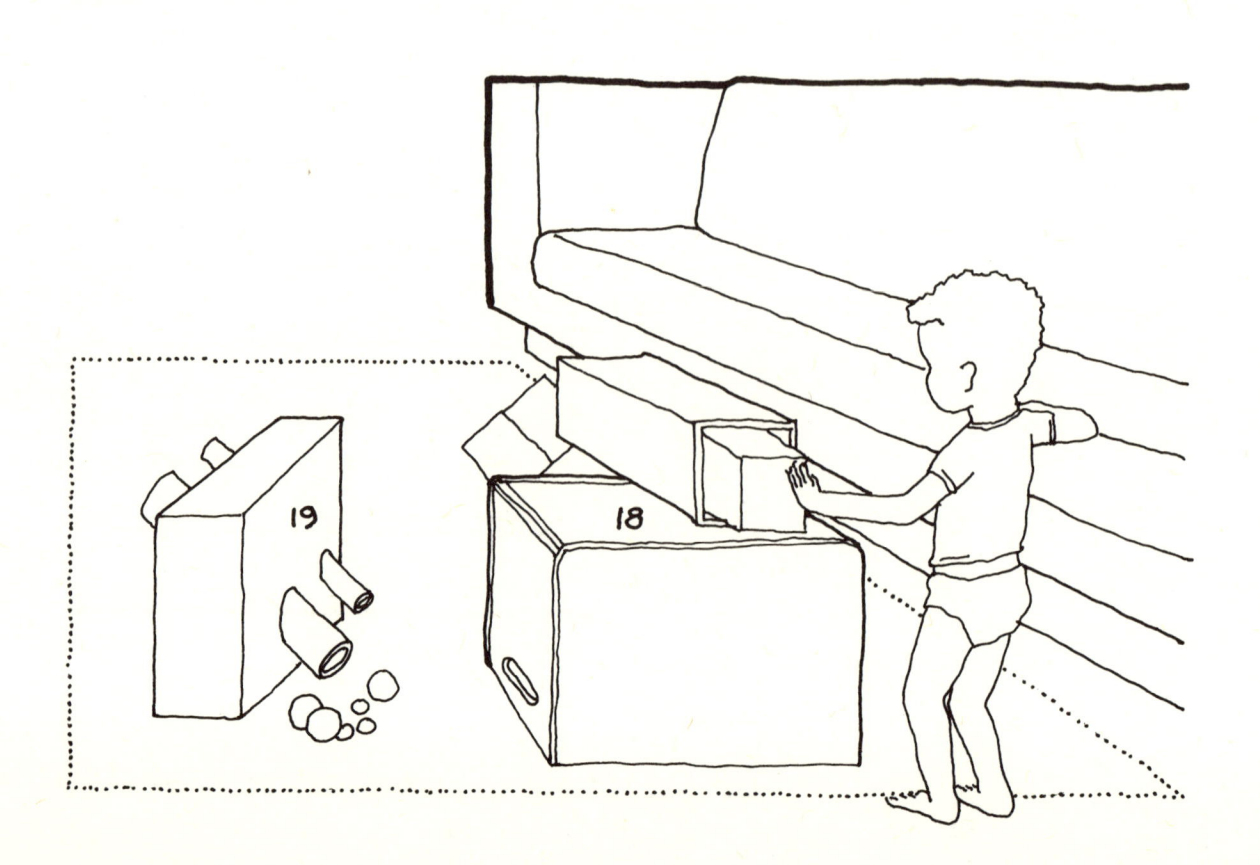

Find five cubical blocks all of the same size. Their dimension determines the size of the tunnel you make of cardboard, which should be just long enough to hold four blocks. When the fifth is pushed in the tunnel, the first falls out the other end. (18)

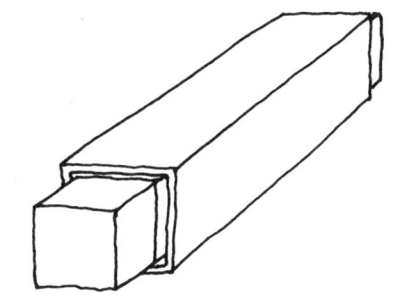

CYLINDER SLIDE

This is similar in some respects to the Push-Through, except that it uses balls instead of blocks, and gravity is responsible for the magical reappearance of the object at the other end. All you need are two sizes of balls, a thinnish carton, and two cardboard tubes — a small one for the small balls and a bigger one for the larger balls. If you have any trouble finding anything larger than a paper towel roll, you can buy mailing tubes, inexpensively, in almost any size you will need. (These are constructed to withstand quite a beating.) For an older child, the Cylinder Slide makes a good competitive game of "whose-goes-farthest," as well as a kind of amateur laboratory for experiments with gravity. (19)

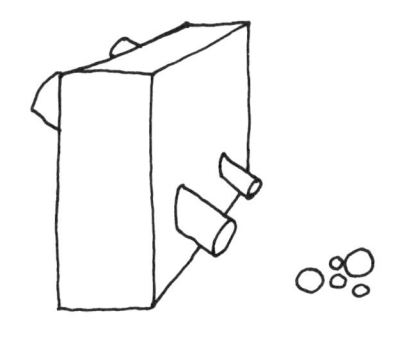

PUSH-THROUGH

Materials
- 1/8" cardboard
- five cubical blocks of equal size
- glue
- colored Con-Tact paper
- fabric tape

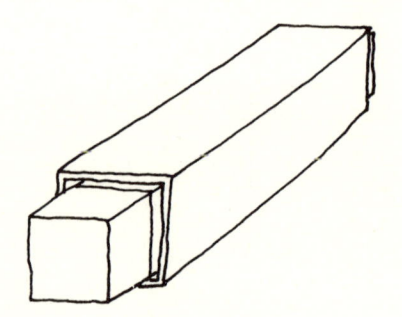

1. Cut out four rectangles of cardboard for inner tunnel. For sizes, use this formula:
   blocks = x" by x" by x"
   cardboard for inner tunnel =
       4x" by x" + 3/8"
2. Glue inner box together as shown and tape along all four edges.
3. Cut out four rectangles of cardboard for outer tunnel. For sizes, use this formula:
   blocks = x" by x" by x"
   cardboard for outer tunnel =
       4x" by x" + 5/8"
4. Glue pieces for outer tunnel to inner tunnel, as shown.
5. Cover tunnel with Con-Tact paper.
6. Tape along joints and around each end.

Inner Tunnel

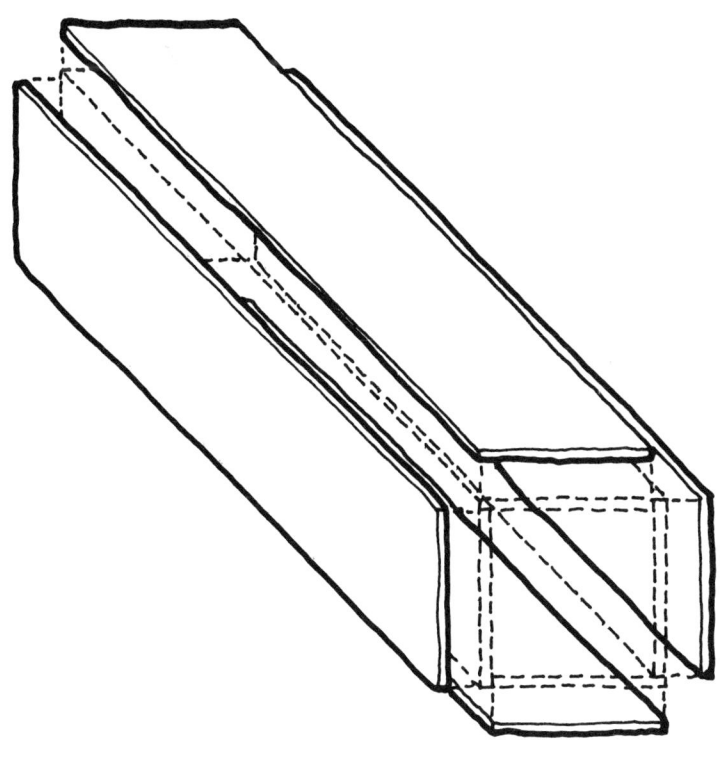

Outer Tunnel

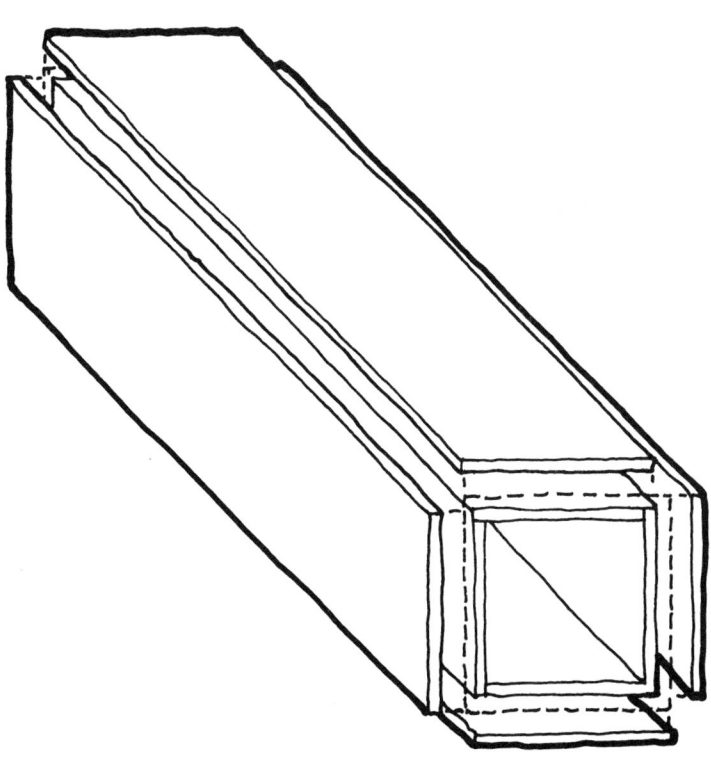

CYLINDER SLIDE

Materials

cardboard carton (approximately 6" by 15" by 15")
collection of balls in two sizes
cardboard tubes in two sizes
fabric tape

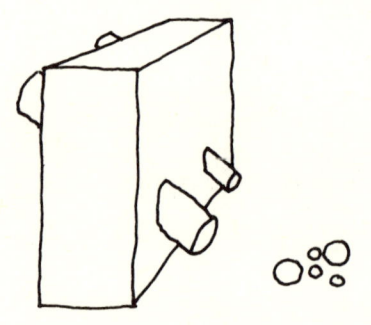

1. Cut ellipses into box where the tubes are to pass through diagonally from the top of one side to the bottom of the other side. (Start with circles the size of the tubes and expand them gradually until the proper ellipse is achieved.)
2. Tape around holes in the box.
3. Tape around the ends of each tube.
4. Put tubes through holes. Tape tubes to holes if they don't fit snugly.

87

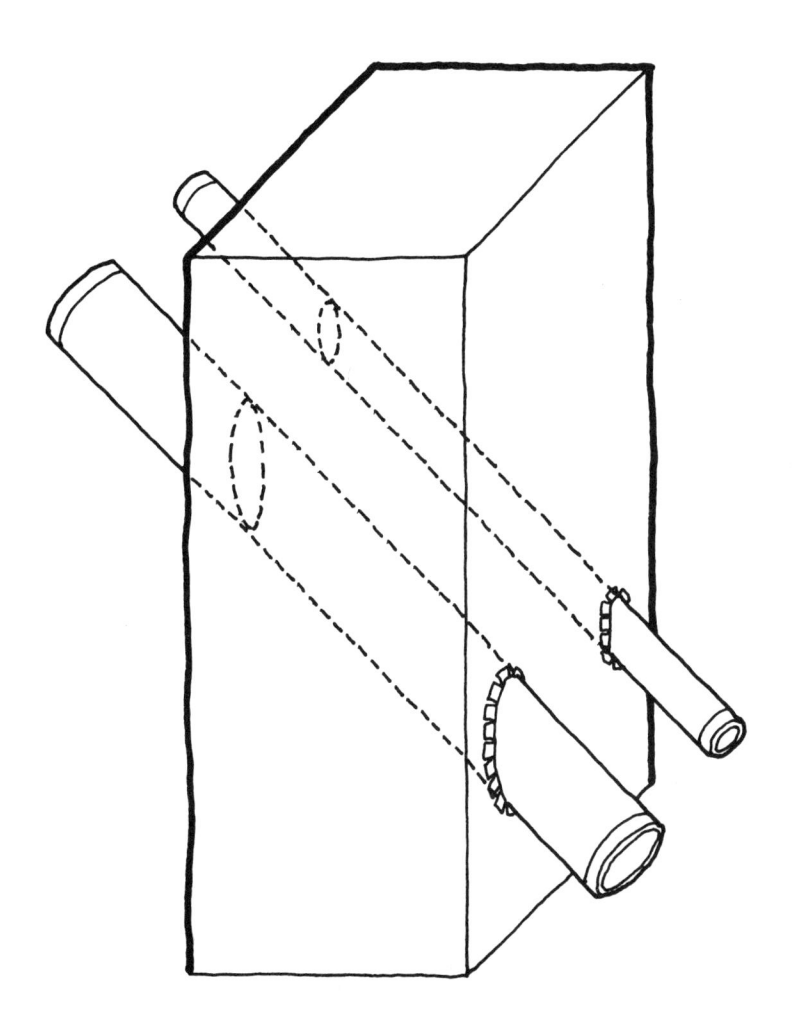

NESTING BOXES

Nesting boxes are a step up in difficulty from nesting jars and cups. I would start out with three, and add two more in between when your child has mastered the first set. You construct them in much the same way you made the shape-sorting box, using the dimensions and procedure shown in the diagram. (20)

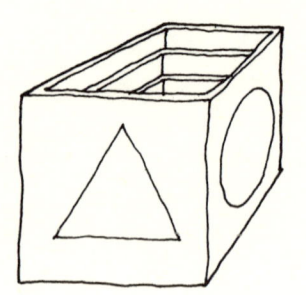

You can transform these into a categorizing puzzle, to be used at an older age, by pasting carefully chosen pictures on the four sides.

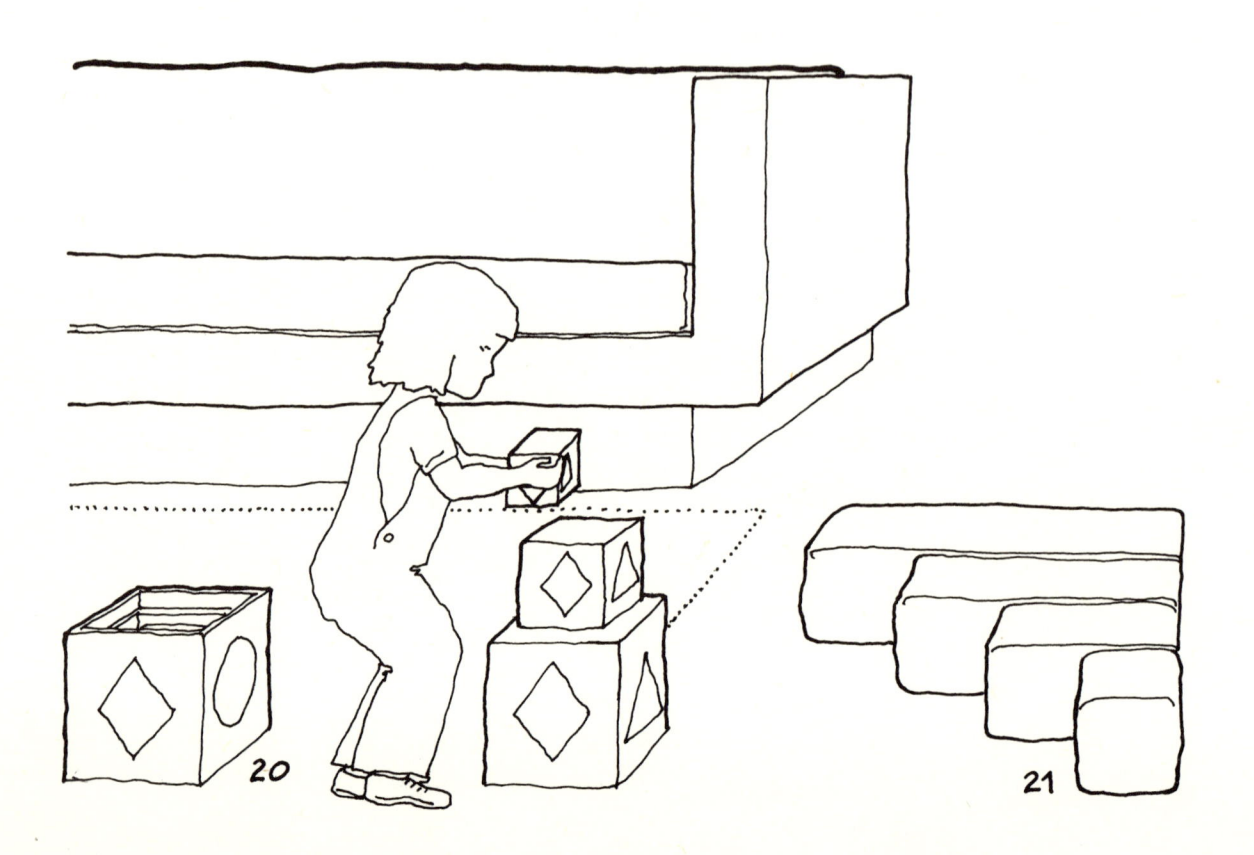

I chose four categories of things to illustrate — animals, plants, wheeled vehicles, and boats. Since there were three blocks, I had three objects in each category, ranging from small to large. For example, in the animal series I used a cat on the smallest box, a horse on the medium sized box, and an elephant on the large box. The vehicle category consisted of a tricycle, a car, and a bus; the boat category consisted of an inner tube, a rowboat, and a sloop; the plant category consisted of a small plant, a shrub, and a tree.

Each category was also color coded — blue vehicles, red boats, green plants, and gray animals — with tape around the top and bottom edges in the same colors, so that Christopher could arrange the blocks in order by color before he was able to sort by categories.

NESTING BOXES

Materials

    1/8" thick cardboard
    glue
    colored Con-Tact paper
        or
    appropriate pictures and clear Con-Tact paper
    fabric tape

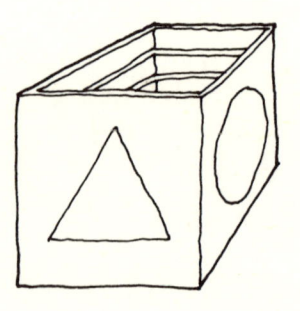

1. Cut out cardboard for inner boxes (see dimensions at right).
2. Glue the four sides and bottom of inner boxes together as shown.
3. Reinforce edges with tape and let dry.
4. Cut out cardboard for outer boxes (see dimensions at right).
5. Glue the four sides and bottom of outer boxes to inner boxes as shown.
6. Cover all three boxes with the same color Con-Tact paper.
        or
Decorate the sides with pictures or designs, as suggested in the text, and cover with clear Con-Tact paper.
7. Tape around all edges.

Sizes of Pieces

6" Box
- inside sides   5 5/8"w by 5 3/4"h
- inside bottom   5 3/4" by 5 3/4"
- outside sides   5 7/8"w by 5 7/8"h
- outside bottom 6" by 6"

4 1/2" Box
- inside sides   4 1/8"w by 4 1/4"h
- inside bottom   4 1/4" by 4 1/4"
- outside sides   4 3/8"w by 4 3/8"h
- outside bottom 4 1/2" by 4 1/2"

3" Box
- inside sides   2 5/8"w by 2 3/4"h
- inside bottom   2 3/4" by 2 3/4"
- outside sides   2 7/8"w by 2 7/8"h
- outside bottom 3" by 3"

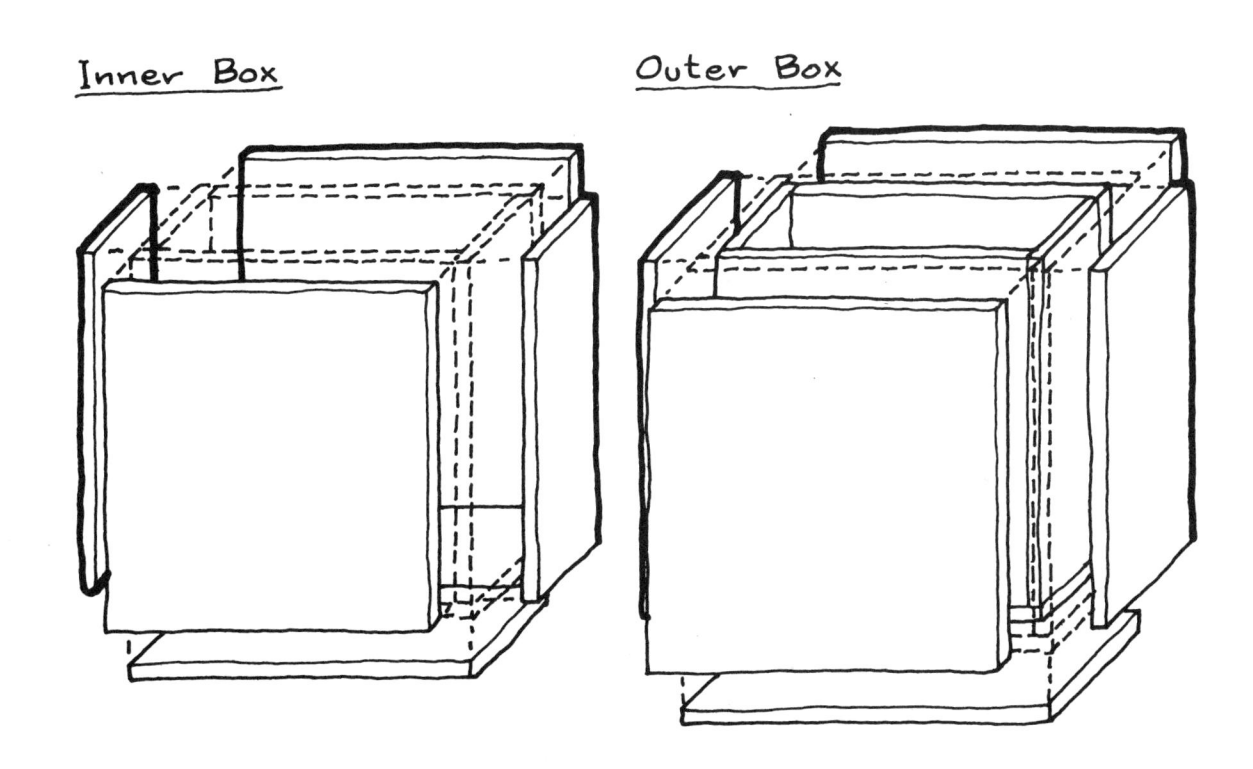

Inner Box

Outer Box

BLOCKS

A one-year-old probably will not build anything very remarkable with blocks, but a child this age will still enjoy stacking a few in a tower and knocking them down. Beginner blocks are simple to make:

- You can make a small set of wooden blocks by sawing up a 2 by 2 into cubes. Sand them and paint them.
- Empty milk cartons make fairly sturdy blocks if you cut off the spout end and fit two inside each other. You can vary the sizes by cutting them in halves or in thirds and by buying milk in various quantities. Empty salt containers can also be used as blocks if you tape them closed.
- Large soft blocks are great for developing the large muscles. Children can sit on them, build towers of them, and throw them about without damaging either themselves or your furniture. I had a few long strips of polyfoam left over after trimming a polyfoam mattress. (I'm sure you can get scraps from a polyfoam store.) I cut them into a graded series using a cube

3" by 3" by 3" as the basic unit. The largest was 3" by 3" by 12". These blocks must be covered with cloth; otherwise your child will chew them to bits. I covered them to correspond to the first four Cuisenaire rods (1-white, 2-red, 3-light green, 4-purple), but you can choose the colors you like. (21)

SOFT BLOCKS

21

Materials
    rectangular solids of polyfoam cloth to cover them (use something sturdy, such as duck cloth)

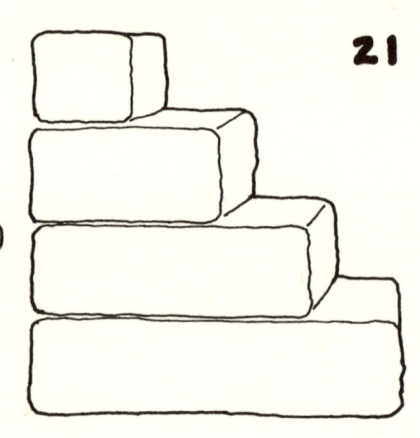

1. Cut rectangular solids of polyfoam or get them pre-cut in the following sizes (several of each size):
3" by 3" by 3"
3" by 3" by 6"
3" by 3" by 9"
3" by 3" by 12"
2. Cut fabric according to typical pattern at the right.
3. Sew blocks together along stitch line, leaving flap on one end to insert polyfoam.
4. Turn right side out and insert polyfoam.
5. Hand-sew the remaining three seams of each block.

Reference to Cuisenaire colors:
1 unit - white, 2 unit - red, 3 unit - light green, 4 unit - purple, 5 unit yellow, 6 unit - dark green, 7 unit - black, 8 unit - brown, 9 unit - blue, 10 unit - orange.

95

1 Unit

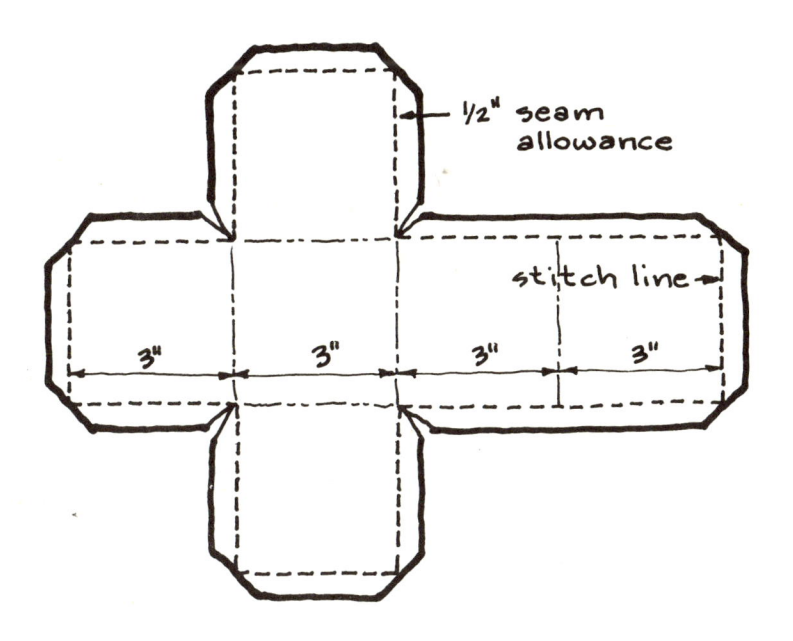

½" seam allowance

stitch line

3" 3" 3" 3"

2 Unit

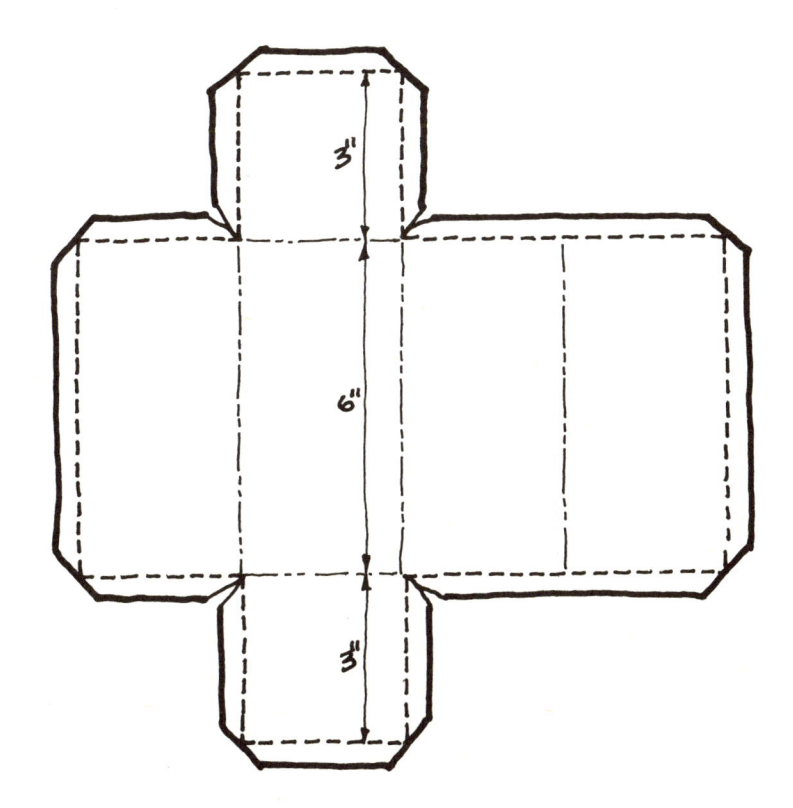

3"

6"

3"

96

PHOTOGRAPH

Push Toy
Pull Toy
Milk Crate Steps
Milk Crate Tunnel
Milk Crate Wagon
Slide
Sand Box

PUSH TOYS AND PULL TOYS

When you see your child pushing chairs and boxes around the floor, you know it is time to think about making a push toy. For a while, children who have just mastered the art of walking like the idea of having something to hold onto. They will still enjoy a push toy later, especially if it makes a noise, and it will help develop both large muscles and overall coordination as they learn to drive it around chairs, tables, and other obstacles.

You can make one fairly easily out of a length of broomstick, wooden dowels, empty film reels, and large washers. You will need an electric drill to make the holes, but if you don't own one you probably have friends who do. (22)

If you attach a cord to the handle with a bead to hold onto, the push toy will double as a pull toy.

A paint roller with an extension handle makes an instant push toy. You need only cut the handle to the right length. When you need peace and quiet, you can slip on the refill cylinder.

A cigar box, or a sturdy box of similar size can be transformed into a pull toy, using a threaded steel rod for an axle and film reels or jar tops for wheels. Wrapping wire around the reels makes them heavier. You will need nuts and washers to hold the wheels on the axles and a length of cord with a bead on the end to pull it with. You may want to attach bells or other noisemakers to the box. This will serve your child as a wagon for some time. You can also transform it into a push toy by cutting a block of wood to fit inside

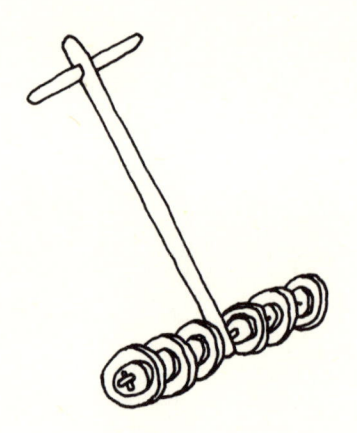

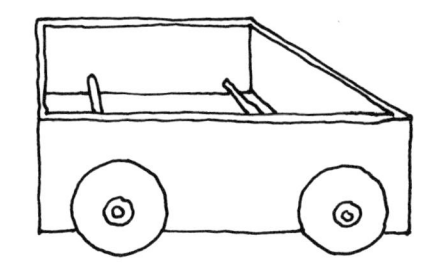

and gluing a length of broomstick
into a hole in the block. (23)

PUSH TOY

Materials

broomstick 24" long

or

3/4" to 1" dowel 24" long

3/8" dowel - one piece 7" long
one piece 10" long

1/8" dowel - four pieces 1½" long

six 8mm (50') film reels

or

six metal jar tops (all the same size)

twelve large washers

1. Drill two 3/8" holes, one in each end of the broomstick or dowel, 1" from the ends.
2. Insert the 7" dowel in the top hole and the 10" dowel in the bottom hole.
3. Lock dowels in place by drilling 1/8" hole perpendicular to and through both the broomstick and the 3/8" dowel.
4. Insert 1/8" dowel and glue them in place.
5. Sand pegs flush with broomstick.
6. Arrange washers and film reels (or jar tops) on the 10" dowel, as shown.
7. Drill and peg each end of axle with 1/8" dowels.
8. Sand down all sharp edges.

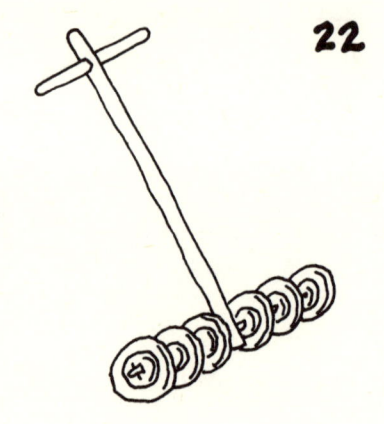

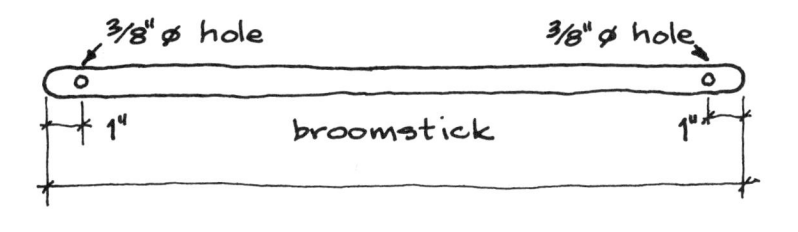

⌀ 3/8" hole   ⌀ 3/8" hole

1"   broomstick   1"

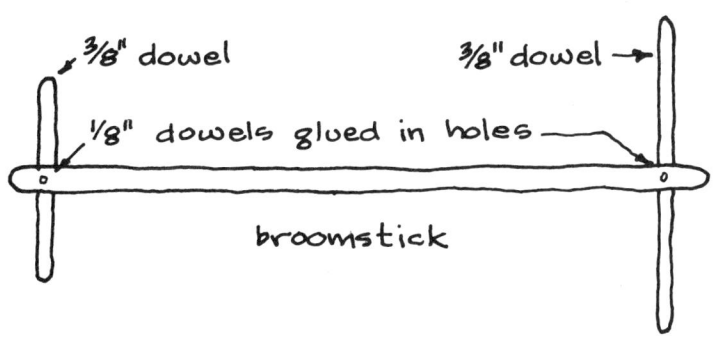

3/8" dowel   3/8" dowel

1/8" dowels glued in holes

broomstick

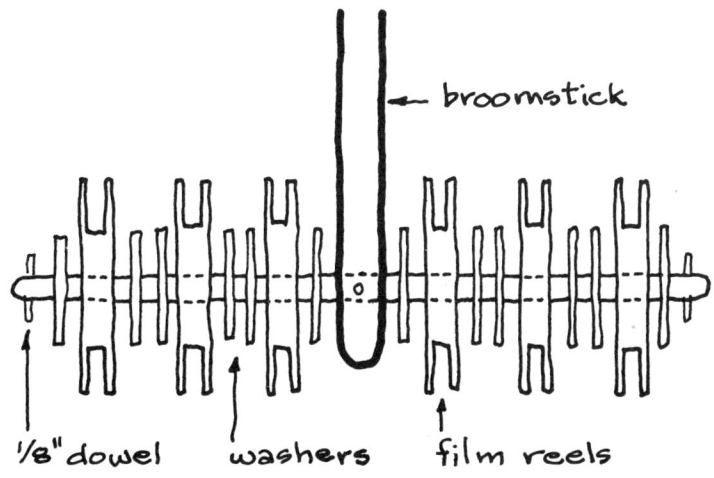

broomstick

1/8" dowel   washers   film reels

PULL TOY

23

Materials

    cigar box (or sturdy box of similar size)
    two pieces 1/4" threaded steel rod 9½" long
    twelve 1/4" washers
    twelve 1/4" nuts

1. Cover box with colored Con-Tact paper if desired.
2. Drill two 1/4" holes in the sides of the box, as shown.
3. Thread a nut and washer on each end of each rod and tighten the nuts against the box, leaving equal amounts of rod on each end.
4. For each wheel use two washers and one film reel, as shown.
5. Thread two nuts on each end of each steel rod and tighten them against each other. (If you use one nut, glue it to the threaded rod.)

To make wagon into a push toy:
1. Cut a block of wood to the inside size of the box.
2. Drill an angled hole in the block to accept a 24" broomstick.
3. Make handle for broomstick, following directions for Push Toy. (22)
4. Glue broomstick into hole in block.

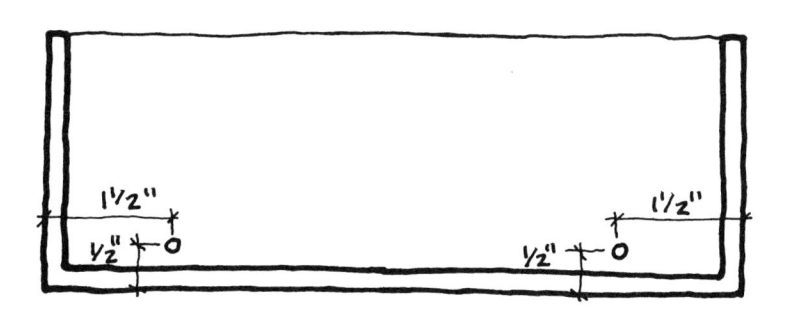

1½" 1½"
½" ○   ½" ○

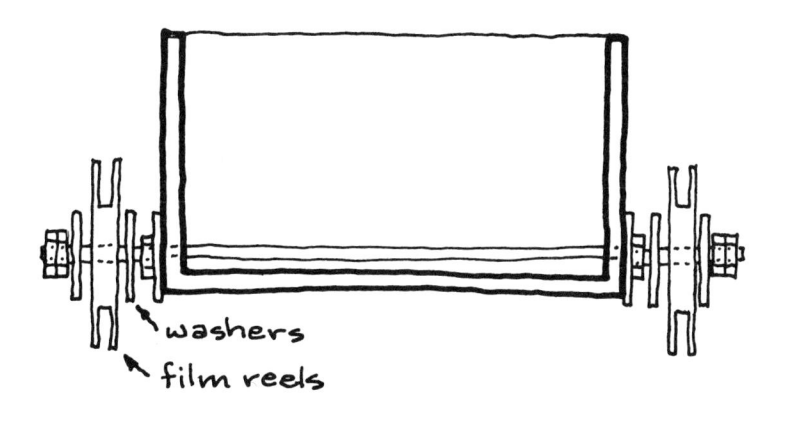

washers
film reels

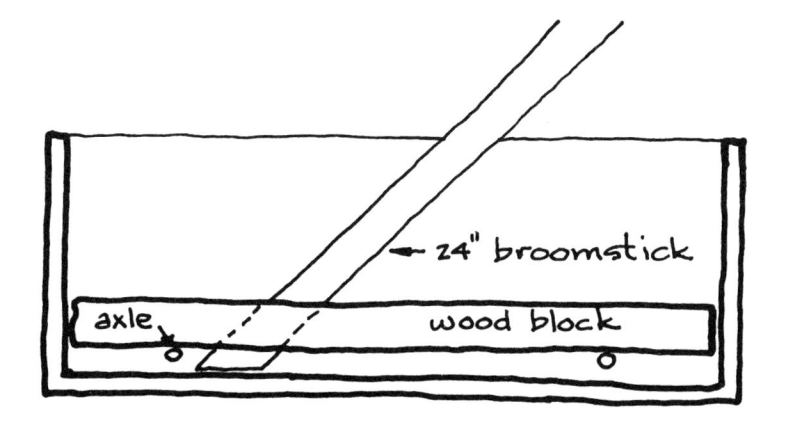

24" broomstick
axle   wood block

OUTDOOR EQUIPMENT

Your child wants a lot of large-muscle activity now. Children approaching eighteen months need space to run in, things to push and pull, places to climb up to, around, and through, large objects to carry, balls to throw, and vehicles to ride. (A simple rider is a basic piece of equipment. Unless you are skilled in carpentry, however, this is something you will have to buy.)

If you have no outdoor space of your own, you take your child to

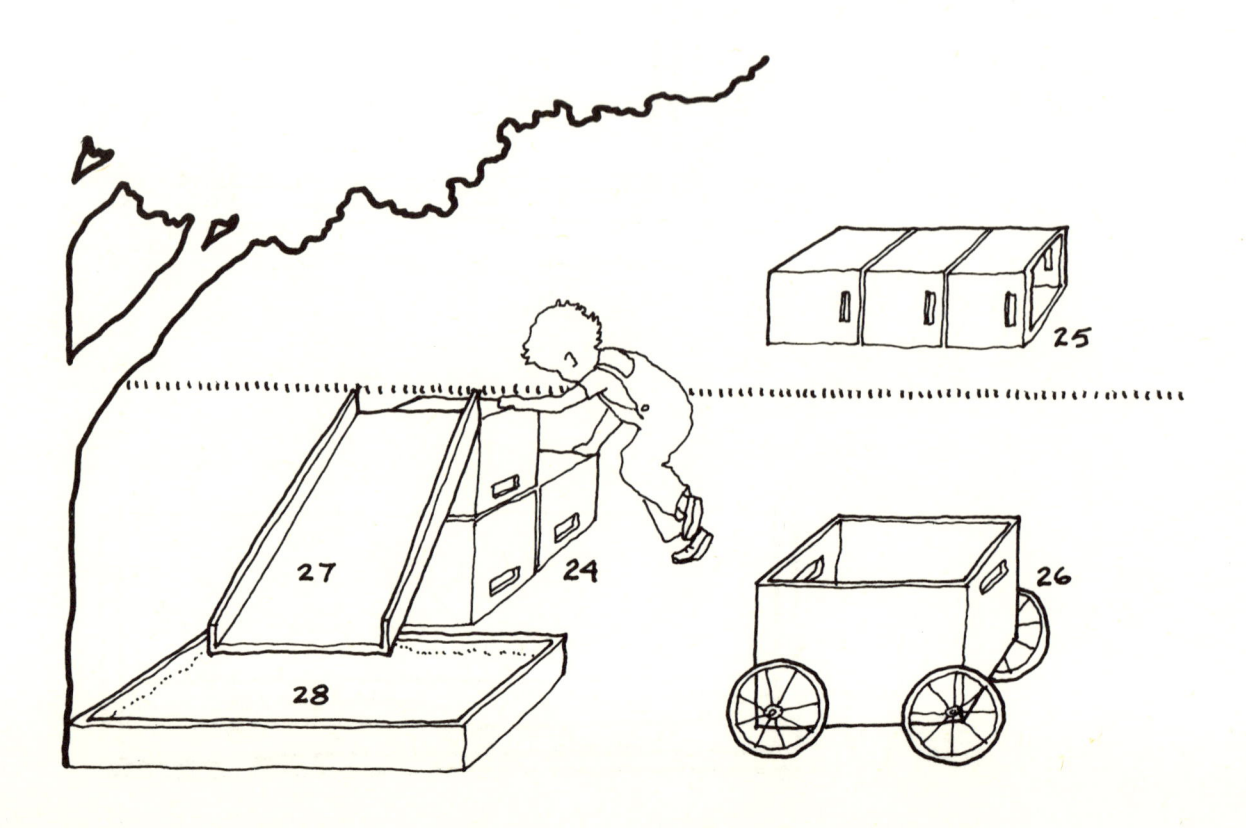

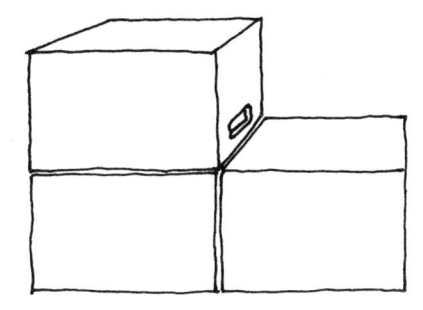

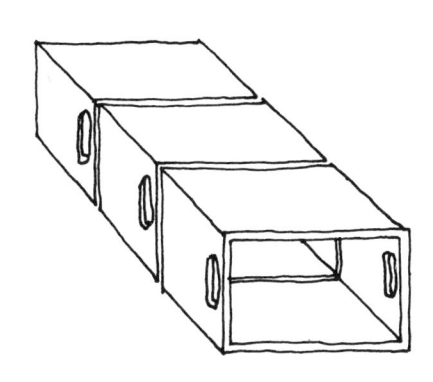

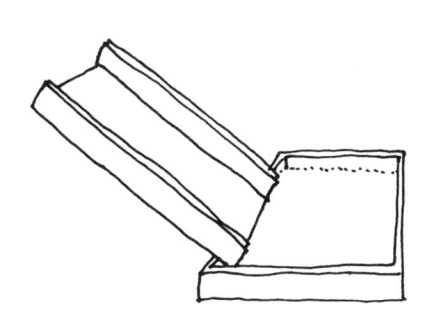

playgrounds. Unfortunately, there are few playgrounds designed for children under two. The slides, swings, and jungle gyms in most playgrounds are not appropriate for a small child and are often dangerous. About all the child can do is play in the sandbox and climb on the park benches. You're lucky if you have your own outdoor space to develop into a suitable environment. Milk crates can be converted into all manner of outdoor equipment. You can:
- Wire them together in steps for climbing. (24)
- Cut out the bottoms and wire them together in a row to form a tunnel. (25)
- Put wheels on them for riding, pushing, and pulling. (26)

You can make a short slide out of sanded, painted boards, ending up in a sandbox, which has been easily constructed from a few boards. (27, 28)

You should provide dirt and water as well as sand. They can be contained in old washtubs, dishpans, or any other large container or bucket. You need not buy special sandbox toys. Old pieces of kitchen equipment — pots, plastic containers, milk cartons, scoops, spoons — are perfectly adequate.

MILK CRATE EQUIPMENT

<u>Materials</u>

    seven plastic milk crates
    plastic coated electrical wire
    threaded steel rod (two pieces about 20" long, diameter to fit wheels)
    nuts and washers (sixteen of each)
    4 wheels (about 6" in diameter)

STEPS

1. Wire milk crates to each other by passing wire through openings in crates and twisting wire with pliers until tight.
2. Tuck ends of wire inside crates leaving no protrusions.

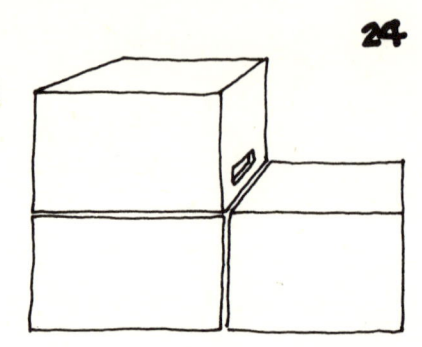

TUNNEL

1. Cut bottoms out of three crates using a sabre saw or a keyhole saw.
2. Wire crates together to form tunnel.
3. Tuck ends of wire into crate recesses leaving no protrusions.

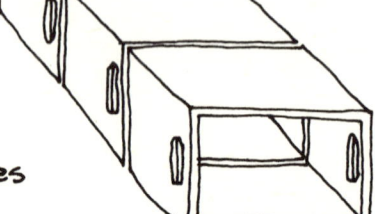

WAGON

1. Drill holes in crate for axles.
2. Pass threaded rods through axle holes positioning nuts and washers as shown at right. Secure to crate by tightening nuts A and B against each other.
3. Slide on wheels and tighten nuts C and D against each other leaving enough play for wheels to rotate.

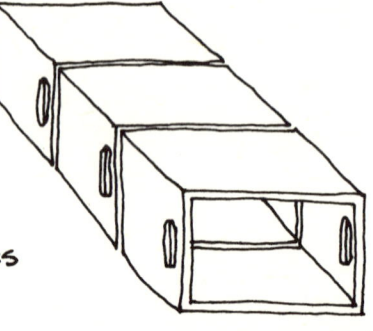

Wagon Wheel Detail

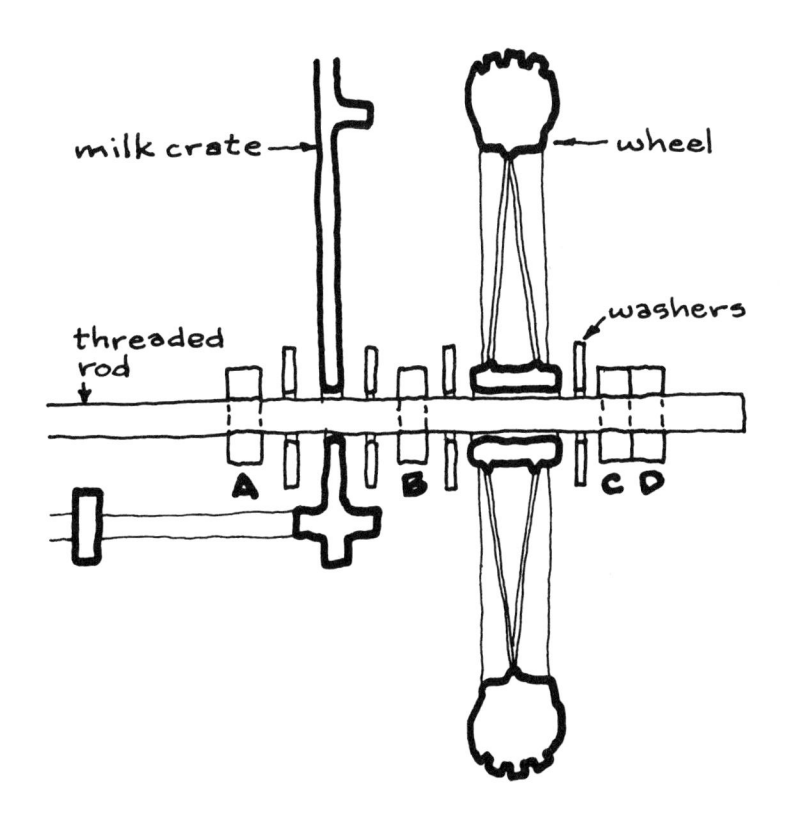

milk crate

wheel

threaded rod

washers

A   B   C D

SLIDE AND SANDBOX 27, 28

Materials
two pieces particle board ¾" thick (36" by 16½" and 34½" by 22½")
four pieces 1" by 4" pine 36" long
two pieces 1" by 4" pine 22½" long
three dozen #10 wood screws 2"
two ¼" by 2½" bolts with four washers and two wing nuts
paint

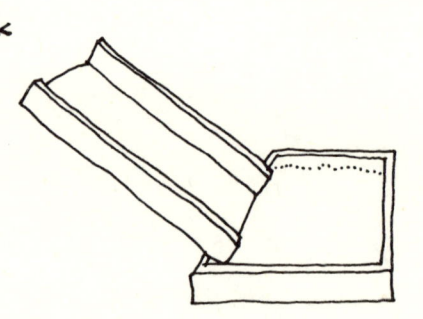

Slide
1. Attach two 36" rails to 36" by 16½" particle board with screws.
2. Drill slide and milk crate steps to accept two bolts (see detail at right).
3. Sand all rough edges and paint.
4. Bolt slide to milk crate steps.

Sandbox
1. Screw sides of sandbox to bottom particle board (34½" by 22½"), as shown at right.
2. Sand edges and paint.

Slide

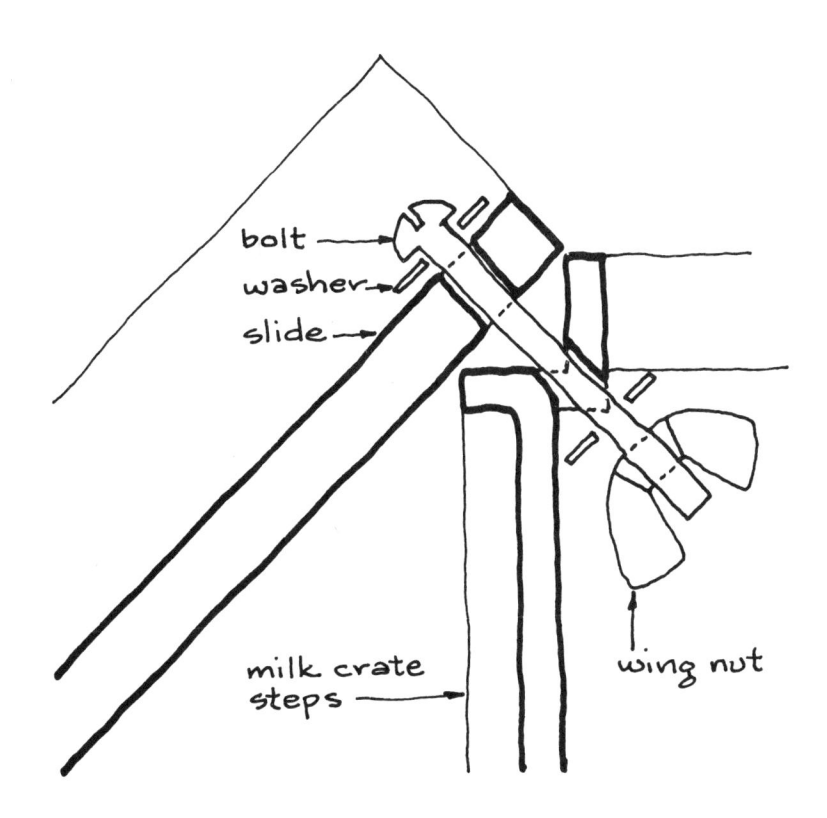

bolt
washer
slide
milk crate steps
wing nut

Sandbox

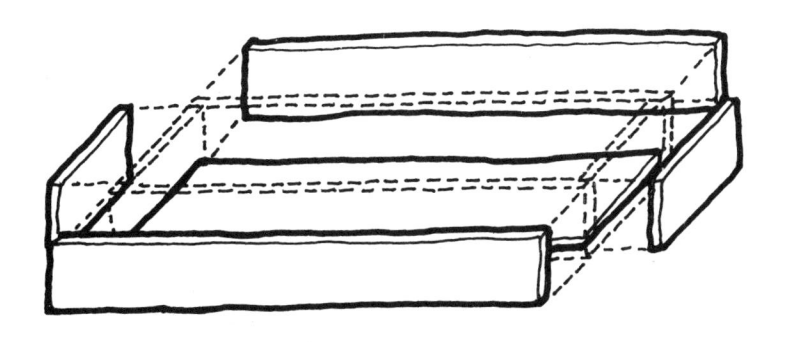

PHOTOGRAPH

Triangular Nesting Boxes
Block Dowel
Bead String
Scrap Puppet
Inset Puzzle

CHAPTER SEVEN

18 MONTHS TO TWO YEARS

In the second half of the second year you may find that you don't need to give your child many new playthings. Your child will still be playing with most of the toys he or she used in the first half of the year but will use them with more dexterity and comprehension.

NESTING TOYS

Your child may be ready for the addition of two more nesting boxes — a 3¾" cube and a 5¼" cube to fit in between the series of three. For variation on the nesting box theme, you can make triangular nesting boxes as well. (29)

STRINGS AND CHAINS

Stringing toys may be appropriate now. You might start out by providing a dowel in a base and blocks with holes drilled in them. (30)

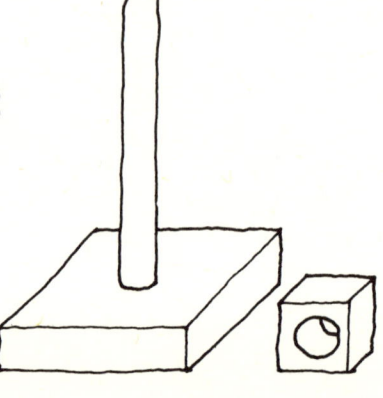

When your child has mastered the basic technique, you can tie a longish piece of thick yarn to a screw eye screwed into the toy shelves close to the floor. Tape the end to make a "needle." (31) This can be used for stringing the drilled blocks or napkin rings. Eventually, your child can move on to stringing beads or spools on a piece of cord.

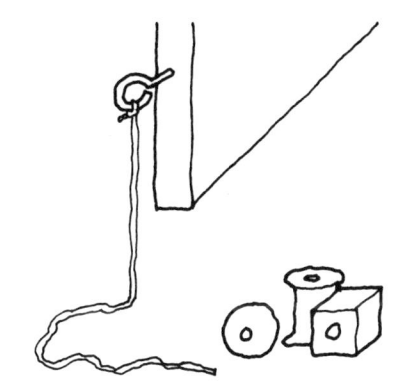

"S" hooks - found in any hardware store - make good chains. Your child can hang them on a screw eye screwed to the shelves at shoulder height. Provide just a few at first. Later your child can make longer chains or use them in conjunction with large rings. He or she can also hook them onto toy cars or trucks and pull them around with a string.

TRIANGULAR NESTING BOXES   29

<u>Materials</u>
　　1/8" thick cardboard
　　glue
　　colored Con-Tact paper
　　fabric tape

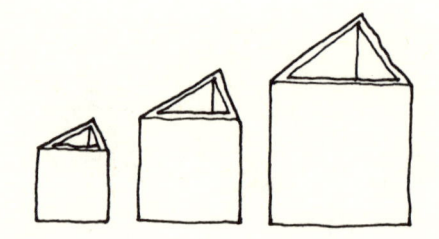

1. Cut out cardboard for inner boxes. (See dimensions at right.)
2. Glue the three sides and bottom of inner boxes together as shown, taping them together as you go.
3. Cut out cardboard for outer boxes. (See dimensions at right.)
4. Glue the three sides and bottom of outer boxes to the inner boxes, as shown.
5. Cover all three boxes with the same color Con-Tact paper.
　　　　<u>or</u>
Use pictures to make a categorizing puzzle as suggested for regular nesting boxes (page 88), and cover with clear Con-Tact paper.
6. Tape around all edges.

Sizes of Pieces

4" Box
- inside sides   3 7/16"w by 3 3/4"h
- inside bottom 3 5/8" by 3 5/8" by 3 5/8"
- outside sides   3 13/16"w by 3 7/8"h
- outside bottom 4" by 4" by 4"

6" Box
- inside sides   5 7/16"w by 5 3/4"h
- inside bottom 5 5/8" by 5 5/8" by 5 5/8"
- outside sides   5 13/16"w by 5 7/8"h
- outside bottom 6" by 6" by 6"

8" Box
- inside sides   7 7/16"w by 7 3/4"h
- inside bottom 7 5/8" by 7 5/8" by 7 5/8"
- outside sides   7 13/16"w by 7 7/8"h
- outside bottom 8" by 8" by 8"

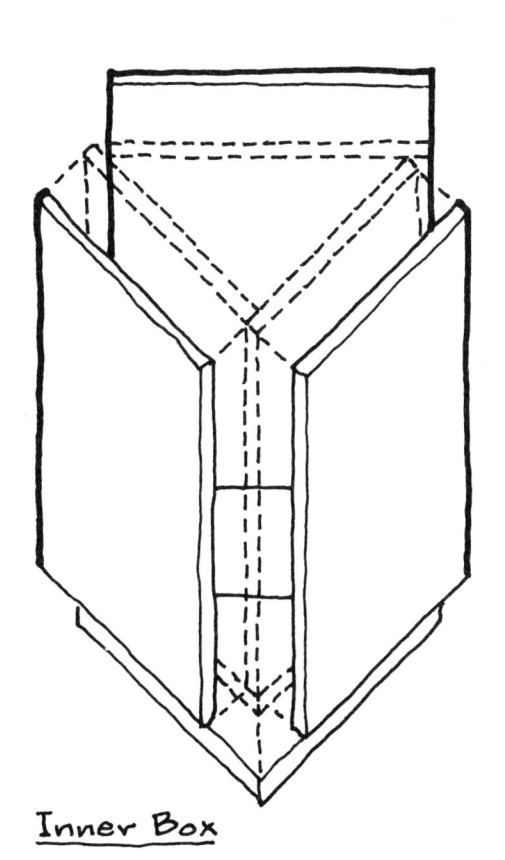

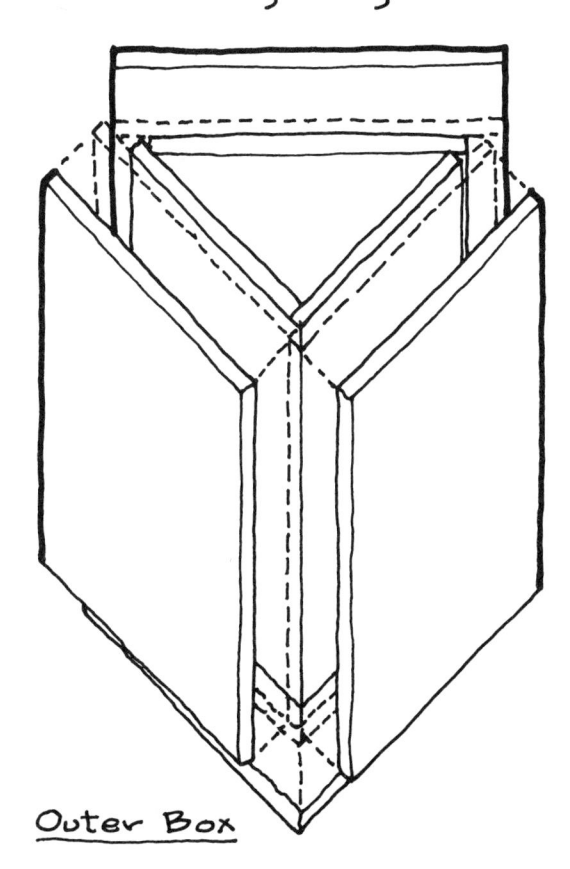

Inner Box   Outer Box

BLOCK DOWEL

30

<u>Materials</u>
wood for base, approximately 4" by 4" by ½" (or cardboard squares laminated together)
½" dowel 8½" long
wood blocks (cubes, spheres, or cylinders) approximately 2" in size

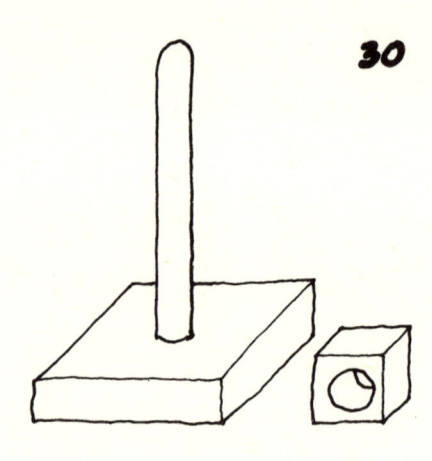

1. Drill ½" diameter hole in center of base.
2. Glue dowel in hole, one end of dowel flush with bottom of base.
3. Drill ¾" diameter holes in blocks.
4. Sand down any sharp edges.
5. Blocks may be painted different colors with enamel paint.

31

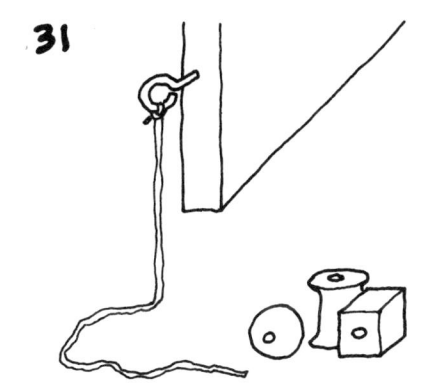

BEAD STRING

<u>Materials</u>
- large screw eye
- tape
- yarn or cord

1. Tape around the end of a length of yarn or cord to make a "needle."
2. Screw a large screw eye to a low shelf.
3. Tie other end of yarn to screw eye.

PUPPETS

You can find out whether your child would enjoy small puppets by giving him or her one of your gloves to play with. If your child likes the idea of putting it on and wiggling it about, you can make a simple puppet using leftover scraps of material and a piece of turned wood for the head. Most children this age can't manipulate the kind of puppet where they have to put a finger in a hole to move the head, but they can manage it if they hold onto a knob inside and let the arms of the puppet dangle.

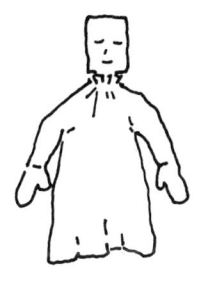

I used a peg person from a toy discarded by another child: its body became the head of our puppet and its head became the knob inside. (32) If you can't find a suitable piece of turned wood for the head around your house, you may be able to find one in a store that sells decorator accessories (including tops for four-poster beds and tie-backs for curtains) or in a scrap bin outside a lumber factory. Alternatively, glue a bead to a small block of wood.

Children's socks are the right size for sock puppets for a small child. All you need to do is decorate a sock appropriately with fringe, vinyl scraps, or whatever, and, perhaps, stuff its nose with cotton.

PUPPET

<u>Materials</u>

    suitable wood block

        <u>or</u>

    two beads glued together

    scraps of material

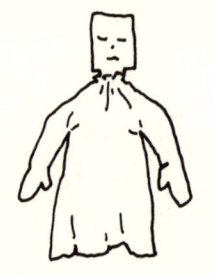

1. Trace around child's hand to ascertain dimensions of puppet (leave plenty of room).
2. Cut and sew fabric for body, leaving opening at neck.
3. Slip the body over the bottom part of the block.
4. Draw the neck together and sew closed.

121

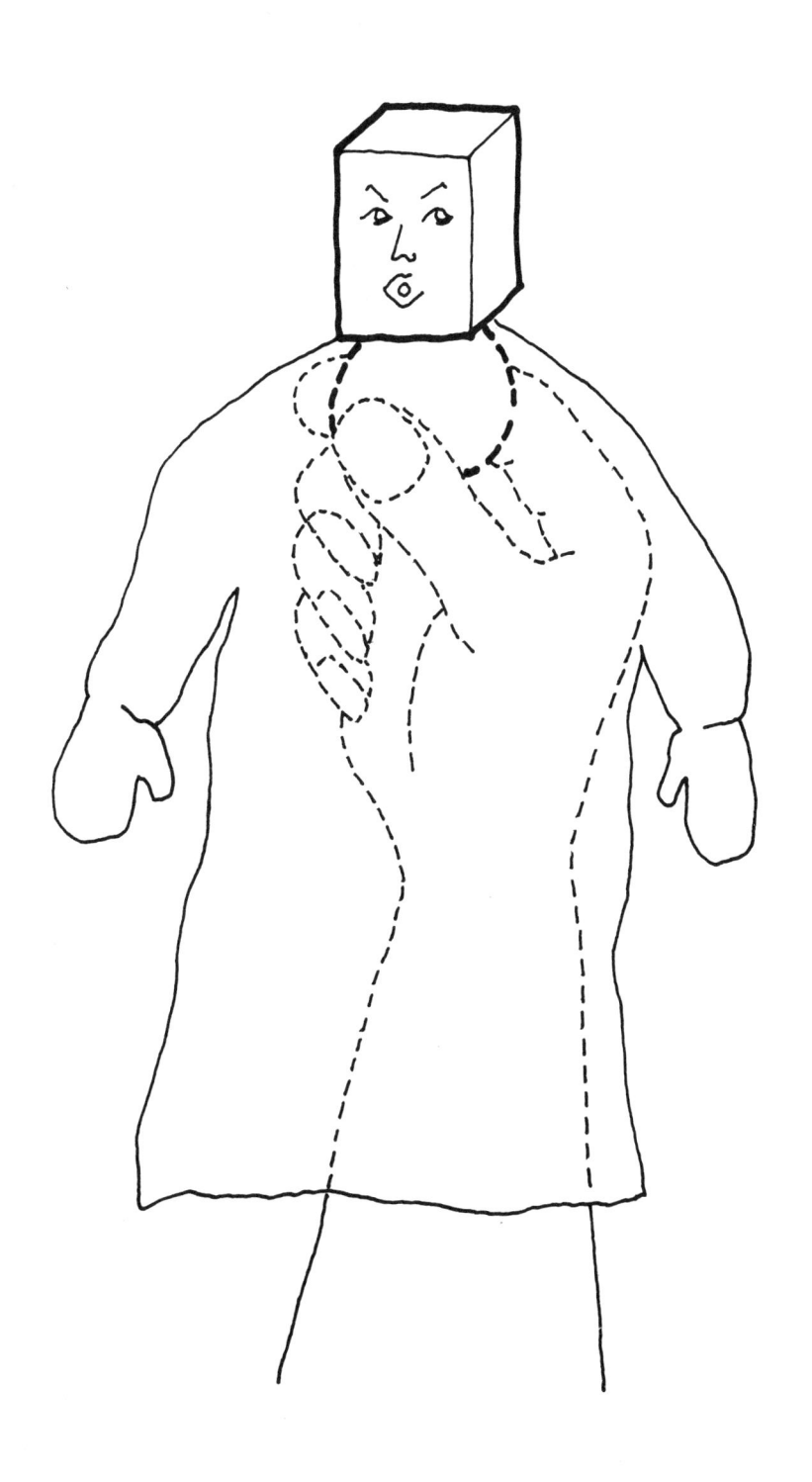

MORE PUZZLES

Jigsaw puzzles, no matter how simple, are probably still too difficult for a child under two. But your child may be able to handle "object puzzles" made with familiar, simple objects. Make a puzzle tray out of laminated cardboard for the objects to fit into. You can use a set of plastic cookie cutters, a set of small bottles, "S" hooks and rings together, or other simple shapes for the puzzle pieces. (33)

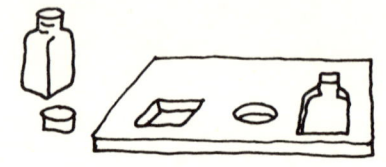

COLOR SORTING GAMES

Differences in color don't seem to interest children until they are around two. The first color games should require differentiation between no more than two contrasting colors.

You can devise a simple color game using the plastic lids from freeze-dried coffee jars. Start with two pairs in contrasting colors, using one large lid and one small lid of each color. Show your child how to put the small one into the large one of the same color.

Pill bottles with colored caps can be used in a somewhat similar way. Your child can put a colored spool or bead into each bottle, then find the matching caps.

Don't forget the color games your child already has:
- colored spools or beads to match
- plastic bottle caps to match
- colored rings to place over colored pegs on a pounding bench

INSET PUZZLE

33

Materials

puzzle objects (set of "S" hooks and rings, or plastic cookie cutters, or plastic bottles and caps)
cardboard
glue
Con-Tact paper (clear or colored)
fabric tape

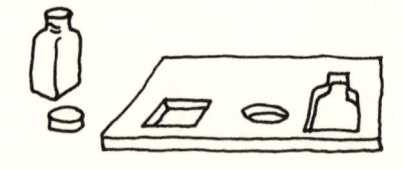

1. Cut out four rectangles of cardboard large enough to accommodate puzzle pieces with space in between and at edges.
2. Cut out holes for objects in three of the cardboard rectangles, about 1/8" larger all around than the objects.
3. Laminate the three rectangles together, lining up holes.
4. Cover the top with Con-Tact paper, including holes, cutting and wrapping the Con-Tact paper around edges of holes.
5. Cover fourth (base) piece of cardboard with Con-Tact paper.
6. Glue three top pieces to base piece.
7. Tape around edges.

Note: Objects like plastic bottles can fit into several different holes, provided that the side, top, and bottom views of the object are different.

125

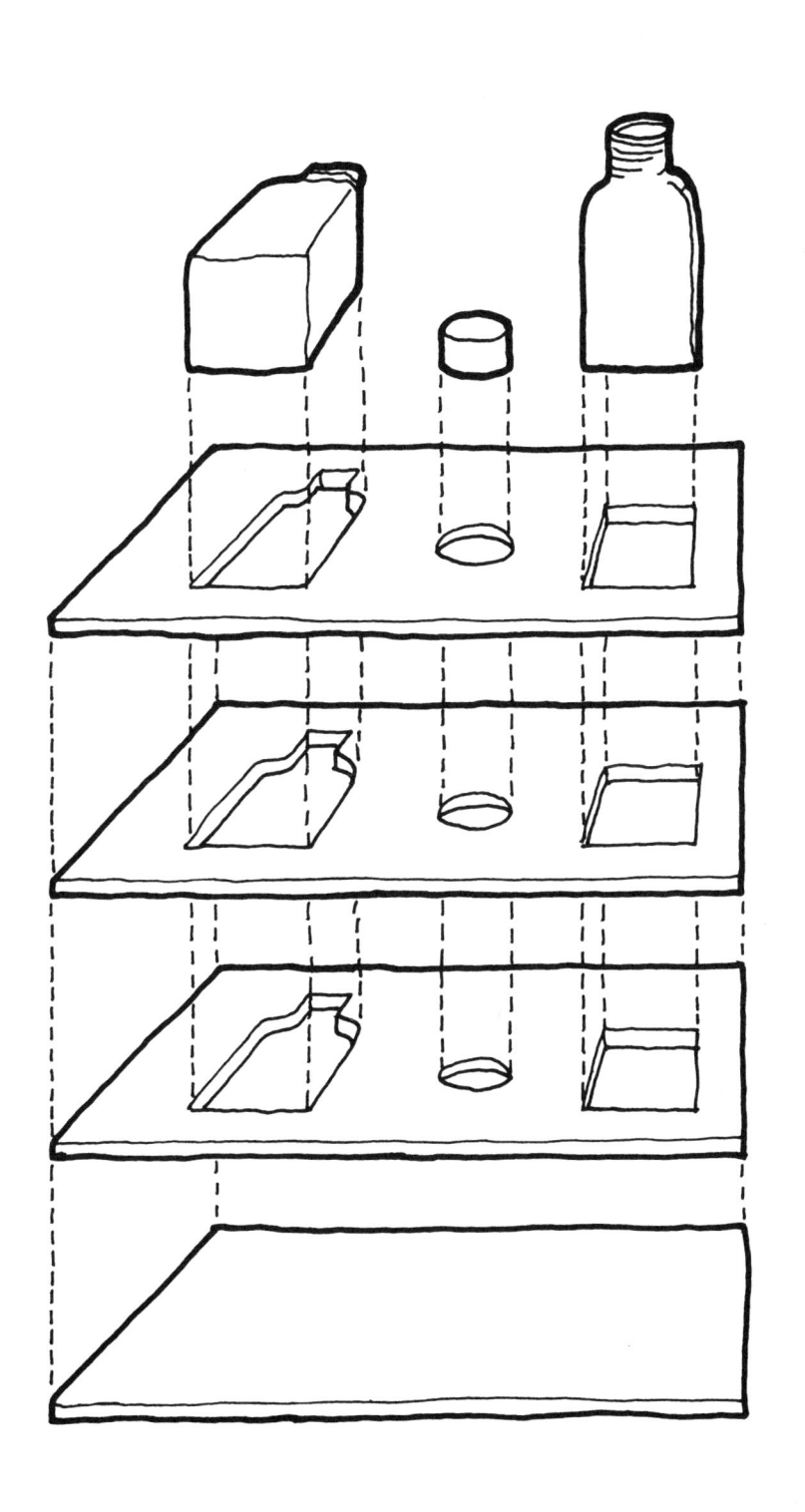

TWO AND BEYOND

After the age of two children's rates of development in various areas become increasingly diversified. It becomes correspondingly more difficult for anyone but you to design or choose appropriate play materials for your child. More than ever, you need to observe your child with care to determine where your child's interests lie and what skills he or she is trying to develop. Once you decide what your child needs, you will discover a wealth of possibilities inherent in all kinds of materials. Eventually, you can begin involving your child in making playthings. Creating them together can become a learning process for both of you.